Coaching Inclusion

"In this timely, accessible, and multi-faceted discussion of inclusive leadership, Dr. Jane Horan draws from a rich well of experience in coaching, research, teaching, and decades of living and working in a variety of countries and contexts. Blending rich and relevant data with artful meditation and hard-earned insight, Horan offers tools for personal and institutional transformation. A deft guide through complex and contentious topics such as generational difference, dual career navigations, and artificial Intelligence and its discontents, Horan challenges us all to imagine and then inhabit a genuinely inclusive leadership landscape."
—Dr Staci Ford, *Lecturer, Gender Studies Programme, The University of Hong Kong.*

"I've had the privilege of knowing and working alongside Jane Horan for many years, and I've always admired her clarity of thought, moral courage, and unwavering commitment to inclusion. In a world where diversity can easily become a corporate slogan, Jane's work consistently brings it back to what truly matters—people, purpose, and performance. Coaching Inclusion is the culmination of years of experience, research, and lived wisdom. Jane offers far more than frameworks—through the Inclusive Leadership Compass powerful tool—she provides a call to action grounded in humility, empathy, and behavioral change. This is not a book that sits on a shelf; it's a guide that challenges us to lead better, coach deeper, and build organizations where everyone has a seat and a say. As someone who works at the intersection of leadership, organizational transformation, and AI, I found the chapters exploring technology's role in inclusive coaching both timely and thought-provoking. Jane doesn't just speak to today's leaders—she anticipates tomorrow's challenges with insight and compassion. I know this, because Jane has served at a key knowledge provider to Catapult- Asia's first dedicated leadership and innovation institute located in Singapore. This book is Jane at her best: thoughtful, incisive, and deeply human. I can't recommend it highly enough to anyone serious about shaping inclusive, high-performing cultures."
—Dr. James R. Andrade *Executive Advisor | Leadership Architect | Advocate for Human-Centered AI, Former Head of Catapult Leadership & Innovation Institute*

"This ground breaking book stands ready to change the lives of every coach-client combination that receives its message. Jane Horan has a keen eye for what topics and published authors are important to her story. She earns credibility through illustrative examples drawn from her own experience. She provides fresh ideas for coaches at all levels of experience. Perhaps most important, she delivers a robust defense of the importance of inclusion in our organizational and political lives. *Coaching Inclusion* can improve our world!"
—Michael Arthur, *Founder, Intelligent Careers Group*

"I first met Dr. Jane Horan over two decades ago. Even then, as a fellow educator in leadership development, I was struck by how she championed inclusive workplaces at a time when few others recognized its importance. Long before inclusion became a corporate buzzword or a point of political contention, Jane was pioneering new approaches to make every voice heard. Over the years, she has become a trusted colleague and friend, and I've watched her ideas influence countless leaders and organizations. Jane understood early on that embracing inclusion isn't just about doing the right thing—it's about unleashing everyone's full potential and driving innovation and growth. *Coaching Inclusion* is the culmination of Jane's decades of research and experience. In this insightful guide, she makes a compelling, evidence-based case that inclusion is more than a moral imperative—it's a strategic advantage. Through data, case studies, and coaching stories, Jane illustrates how leaders who foster inclusive cultures unlock greater creativity, team engagement, and improved business performance. What I find especially powerful is how Jane blends her academic rigor with practical coaching techniques. She presents a clear framework for leaders to follow, complete with reflective questions and actionable exercises in each chapter. It's like having an executive coach and a professor of leadership rolled into one, guiding you step by step toward becoming a more inclusive leader. This book comes at a crucial time when nearly every company talks about the importance of diversity, yet *Coaching Inclusion* cuts through the buzzwords and gets to the heart of true inclusion. Jane challenges aspiring leaders and HR professionals to move beyond token gestures and build cultures where everyone genuinely belongs and contributes. Her message is clear: inclusion is not a box to check but a daily practice and mindset. She shows that when leaders coach with inclusion in mind, they cultivate more innovative, resilient, and adaptable teams. For HR practitioners, leadership coaches, and managers, the book offers a roadmap for creating workplaces where diverse talent thrives and drives organizational success. Reading *Coaching Inclusion* feels like sitting down with a wise mentor who not only shares stories and research but also cares about your growth as a leader. Jane's voice comes through with warmth and an unwavering conviction in the power of inclusion. As I turned each page, I could sense the decades of experience behind her advice and her genuine enthusiasm for helping others succeed. By the end, I was not only convinced that inclusive leadership drives innovation and business outcomes—I was inspired to put these principles into practice in my own work. It's rare to find a book that is both intellectually rigorous and deeply heartfelt. *Coaching Inclusion* is exactly that, and it stands out as a must-have manual for anyone committed to building better leaders, better teams, and a better future. I whole heartedly endorse Jane Horan's work and this outstanding book. The book will leave you convinced that inclusion is the ultimate catalyst for innovation, and Jane gives you the tools to make it a reality in your organization."

—Drew Boyd, *Author and Global Thought Leader on Innovation and Creativity*

"Dr. Jane Horan's *Coaching Inclusion* is a highly transformative read that challenges leaders to show up with greater courage, empathy, and intentionality. Rather than simply contributing to the inclusion dialogue, this book reshapes it entirely. Grounded in rigorous research, rich global leadership insights, and authentic workplace narratives, Jane makes a compelling case: inclusion isn't a corporate catchphrase—it's a behavior, a mindset, and above all, a daily practice. Packed with practical tools for reflection, adaptation, and action, *Coaching Inclusion* speaks to the real challenges leaders face. The scenarios are not theoretical—they're honest, relatable, and deeply human. Whether you're a senior executive, team leader, or coach, this book is your essential guide to building trust, shifting culture, and enhancing performance in a world where inclusion is not optional—it's a strategic imperative. What resonated most with me is the deep humanity woven through every chapter. Jane redefines leadership as inclusive, measurable, and sustainable—and she offers the roadmap to get there. A globally respected expert with extensive cross-cultural experience, Jane has created more than a must-read - *Coaching Inclusion* is a must-use."

—Sandhya Karpe. *Ph.D. Leader: Asia Human Capital Center & Program Director: Asia CHRO & Inclusion Councils. The Conference Board*

Jane Horan

Coaching Inclusion

Empowering Behaviours for Positive Change

Jane Horan
The Horan Group
Singapore, Singapore

ISBN 978-981-95-0264-6   ISBN 978-981-95-0265-3 (eBook)
https://doi.org/10.1007/978-981-95-0265-3

© The Editor(s) (if applicable) and The Author(s), under exclusive license to Springer Nature Singapore Pte Ltd. 2026

This work is subject to copyright. All rights are solely and exclusively licensed by the Publisher, whether the whole or part of the material is concerned, specifically the rights of translation, reprinting, reuse of illustrations, recitation, broadcasting, reproduction on microfilms or in any other physical way, and transmission or information storage and retrieval, electronic adaptation, computer software, or by similar or dissimilar methodology now known or hereafter developed.
The use of general descriptive names, registered names, trademarks, service marks, etc. in this publication does not imply, even in the absence of a specific statement, that such names are exempt from the relevant protective laws and regulations and therefore free for general use.
The publisher, the authors and the editors are safe to assume that the advice and information in this book are believed to be true and accurate at the date of publication. Neither the publisher nor the authors or the editors give a warranty, expressed or implied, with respect to the material contained herein or for any errors or omissions that may have been made. The publisher remains neutral with regard to jurisdictional claims in published maps and institutional affiliations.

Cover illustration: Contributor:steeve-x-art

This Palgrave Macmillan imprint is published by the registered company Springer Nature Singapore Pte Ltd.
The registered company address is: 152 Beach Road, #21-01/04 Gateway East, Singapore 189721, Singapore

If disposing of this product, please recycle the paper.

Acknowledgements It takes a village to write a book, and believe me, I've liberally tapped into that village of experts.

Writing *Coaching Inclusion: Empowering Behaviours for Positive Change* has been a journey, shaped by conversations, questions, pauses, and encouragement. As John O'Donohue reminds us:

"The universe is full of differences. No two stones or flowers or faces are ever the same."

I am deeply grateful to the leaders, advisors, colleagues, friends and family who shared their insights, time, and trust. Your honesty and generosity shaped every chapter. In listening to your stories, O'Donohue's words reverberated:

"There is such an intricate tapestry of differentiation in even the simplest places. There can be no true self without the embrace of the other."

To those who listened when I was uncertain, challenged when it was needed and quietly cheered me on, thank you. You have reminded me that inclusion is not only a practice, but a way of seeing and being with others.

Early Readers and Thought Partners

My gratitude to those who have contributed at different moments in this book's development, from the earliest seeds to the chapters taking shape and form.

In the nascent stages when my ideas were still percolating, I'm grateful to Staci Ford, PhD and Elizabeth Montgomery, PhD for their engagement and clarity with the preview chapter and its early framing.

As the book -and my thoughts - evolved, Amy Balmuth, Irene Tsang, and Christina Yother, PhD offered close attention, thoughtful comments and honest reflections which immeasurably shaped the flow and narrative.

Guides and Mentors

Throughout the journey, I was fortunate to be accompanied by guides and mentors whose engagement challenged my thinking around inclusion:

James Andrade, PhD, Sandy Sable, PhD, Berndette Dixon and the ILC team, Michael Arthur, PhD, Drew Boyd, Jim Howard, Hayden Majajas, Melanie Coate, Anne Abraham, David Fox, Sandhya Karpe, Sarah Bond, Jin-Theng Craven, Tomi Bryan, PhD, Angel Cheung-Horenfeldt, Colin Duff, Ann Jameson, and Satoshi Hirose.

Community Leadership

Thank you to Mary Lou Weaver Houser and Kyle Gott for offering time, insights, and perspective on building inclusive communities.

Influences and Inspiration

To Nancy Kline, whose Thinking Environment has greatly shaped my writing, listening, and advisory work for many years- my most sincere thanks. And to the global Thinking Environment faculty, especially Candice Smith and Hazel Morley, I'm grateful for your support and models of practice.

Friends from the Global Village

None of this would have remotely been the same without the support and shared energy of these groups:

The Wonky Walkers (Marlene Han, Rie Rumito), The Canoe Academy (Beatrice Mallon, Nicole Reeve, Denes Szaszak), the Singapore Paddling Club, and the N. Mary Street Gang. Thank you all for your movement, laughter, embrace and encouragement.

Family

To Neal, Hank, Elah, and Hertha—thank you for giving me the space to write, even when deadlines loomed, and encouraging me to take that last mile. For everything, I'm grateful.

Competing Interests The author has no competing interests to declare that are relevant to the content of this manuscript.

Introduction—Charting the Path to Inclusion

There's only one way to see things, until someone shows us how to look at them with different eyes
Pablo Picasso

Always There, Rarely Seen

After a few discussions with the Singapore Paddling Club, I brought my mother-in-law to Sentosa Beach early one Saturday morning. She's an avid kayaker and she knows the water well. But I wanted her to experience something new: the warm climes of Singapore, the energy of the paddling community, and the view of the city from the churning waters of the Singapore Straits, where cargo ships and ferries pass on their way between the Pacific and Indian Oceans.

A sticky humid morning with families on the beach, the smell of coconut oil lingered. Jet-skiers raced up to the dock, the waves wobbled the stand-up paddlers. As the morning heat increased, a few put towels down under the shaded spots of the palms. Sipping iced coffee and chatting between training sessions, it was a typical weekend until something made people stop and stare.

Our 1.8-meter-tall coach walked slowly across the sand, holding the hand of my 1.5-meter-tall mother-in-law. The contrast was impossible to miss. He towered over her, his long strides naturally slowing to match her measured steps. Yet, despite the stark height difference, there was something fluid and connected about their movements, his steady presence, her quiet confidence. He bent slightly to listen as she spoke, their conversation appearing both deliberate and easy.

I watched as they reached an OC2, a two-person canoe. She climbed in first, her movements careful but assured. He followed, balancing the boat as they prepared to launch. Then, with one smooth push, they were off, paddling toward the Straits, though still within the boundaries of the blue buoys.

I stood watching, shielding my eyes from the sun. Would she enjoy it? Would she feel that same sense of belonging I had when I first started paddling? I wanted her to feel the same inclusivity as I felt.

The beach carried on as usual, but my eyes kept drifting back to the water, tracking their canoe as it disappeared into the distance. Later, as they made their way back to shore, I walked closer. As they landed, my coach stepped out first and turned to a group of college students nearby, paddles in hand, waiting for their turn.

Then, to my surprise, he raised his voice.

"*Pay attention, everyone,*" he called out, gesturing toward my mother-in-law, still seated in the canoe. "*She's 97 years old and just completed an ocean paddle.*"

A ripple of surprise ran through the group.

"*Wait, 97?!*" one student blurted out, looking around as if they had misheard.

I watched them take it in—the disbelief, then admiration crossing their faces.

"*Yes, 97,*" my coach repeated with a smile. "*So, now, listen up. If she can do it, so can you.*"

The students and everyone on the beach applauded. My mother-in-law, sitting in the canoe, smiled, steadied herself and climbed out, as graceful as ever.

I stood back, taking it all in. I brought her to Sentosa to share something I loved, but I never expected it to become something bigger.

Later that day, as I scrolled through Instagram, I saw that the moment had taken on a life of its own.

'Today our newest member, at 97 years young!'

'Saw her on the water in an OC2. I was so inspired to see this little power engine move that I just had to put in a little more effort myself.'

'Love the balance we see in the club, from the young ones with disabilities all the way to 97-year-old paddlers.'

And then this one:

'This made me rethink how we can include more people in our community, no matter their age or ability.'

That was it. Inclusion wasn't just an idea it was a feeling. A shift in perception.

That morning, people saw my mother-in-law not as "old" but as capable, strong, and fully part of the community. They saw her, and maybe, in doing so, they saw their own potential differently.

A picture of the two of them together captures this contrast even better than words ever could. The towering presence of our coach beside her small but determined frame speaks volumes about the moment of quiet determination and mutual respect.

It wasn't just about her age. It was about what inclusion looks like in action. Or perhaps, more importantly, what inclusion can actually feel like. Those on the beach felt it, as I did, and saw our coach and my mother-in-law through a different prism, a more inclusive one. Its effect was stronger than I imagined.

Outrigger canoeing was originally just a way of life, essential for fishing and trade from island to island. But I found that it embodied inclusion in its purest form not only through this moment but from the day I started paddling. A few years earlier, I had joined a women's team as a novice. From my first paddle, I felt like I belonged, from the encouragement of the coaches to the welcoming of the experienced paddlers.

The coaching was always positive, focused only on improvement rather than what was being done wrong. "*Try to adjust your stroke slightly. You'll feel the difference.*" It wasn't just about holding the paddle more efficiently it was about creating a space where everyone had a purpose and a role to play. Even when I was away for an extended time, the welcome back was always "*Glad you're here.*"

Team sports aren't necessarily meant to showcase inclusion, as everyone knows their role on the team. For me, paddling exemplified inclusion. The coach, the steersperson, or even the paddler in seat three, whose role is to help maintain the rhythm and provide consistent power, recognize each other's unique strengths. Every stroke, every paddle, becomes a collective effort and a reminder that inclusion isn't just something we talk about. It's something that makes all the difference, whether paddling furiously or on land.

Moments like these are nuggets of truth, often overlooked in the course of the day: we are not isolated individuals, but a connected member of our communities, whether that is a team, an organization, a neighborhood, or something larger. Over the next eleven chapters, we'll look at the behaviors of inclusion and grapple with the word's definition in 2025. But in that moment on the beach, I experienced, as did others, what it felt like to be included and acknowledged. In writing this book and thinking back on that experience, I wondered, *how can we bring the inclusive outrigger canoe into the workplace?*

This is where coaching inclusion begins. My goal in writing this book is to help others see the potential in everyone, the way they saw a 97-year-old woman take to the seas.

Contents

Part I Foundations of Inclusion

1 Why Inclusion Matters in Leadership and How Coaching Can Help Develop It   3

2 The Hidden Cost of Exclusion: The Silent Disruptor   11

Part II Building Inclusive Leadership

3 The Inclusive Leadership Compass Framework   23

4 Empathy in Action Leading Inclusive Teams   39

5 Leading with Humility   49

Part III Inclusive Systems and Career Pathways

6 Addressing Inclusion Gaps in Organisational Systems   67

7 Supporting Mid-to Late Career Professionals   89

8 Inclusive Careers for Dual-Career Couples   109

Part IV Driving Cultural Change

9 Building Sustainable Inclusion Through Culture Change   131

Part V Technology and Leadership Insights

10 Leaders' Perspectives on Inclusion, Coaching, and AI   155

11 AI-Powered Tools for Coaching Inclusion   175

Conclusion: Empowering Change—Coaching
for an Inclusive Future   185

References   199

Index   211

PART I

Foundations of Inclusion

CHAPTER 1

Why Inclusion Matters in Leadership and How Coaching Can Help Develop It

To see the World in a Grain of Sand
William Blake

I've started this book many times.
　Personal and professional events, along with ever-changing political, commercial and global events made me wonder whether the world needs another book on coaching, inclusion and more leadership conversations.
　I erased more pages than not at the outset but stopped soon after. As I look at my work with leadership teams in organizations, my coaching engagements and the seismic workplace changes, the answer is a clear yes—the book is indeed needed, a relevant read for present and future organizations.
　Leadership must always be reevaluated and refined, as it is never static, always fluid. To update leadership, we have to reframe the traditional "one-size-fits-all" approach to leadership development, talent selection and organizational programs, as they no longer accurately address the complexities of today's workplace.
　The first step is to acknowledge that the one sitting across the table from you has unique potential for the organization, and to withhold the 'let's see what's wrong' attitude.
　Second is to understand what 'leading inclusively' means and how to support an effective inclusive program. A preliminary definition of inclusive leadership often tilts towards how one honors, respects and elevates

others, raising our humanity and that of others. When humanity integrates into corporate culture, it positively shapes values, fairness and integrity and better aligns business objectives.

I've been fortunate over the course of my career to have worked with leaders through the commercial spectrum. I've coached executives moving into new leadership positions and researched leadership across cultures. I worked for a transformational leader who inspired me and others to do much more than we ever thought possible. Conversely, I've coached transactional leaders who perceived leadership to be a functional exchange of tasks and deliverables, many of whom often lose touch with their co-workers through their task-making.

I studied transformational leadership for my doctoral dissertation, a framework rooted in ethics, values and motivation of others. While transformational leadership knows no gender, my research showed that women consistently had one core attribute and behaviour more than men. What was it? Coaching.

When I asked women leaders across Asia to 'tell me about your leadership style?' almost all said, "I'm not a leader. I'm a coach, facilitator or mentor." That succinctly summed up what was missing—and what is now needed—in leadership.

Transformational leadership is steeped in ethics and values, encompassing attributes such as vision, charisma, inspiration and intellectual stimulation, qualities which motivate teams to exceed expectations. It involves behaviors like individualized consideration, challenging assumptions and encouraging creativity, which bring such attributes to life.

There is great value in active listening, nurturing growth in others and building a sense of community, along with a leader's values, innate tendencies and mindset.

Interviewing women for my research, I saw "purpose-driven" leadership, which concentrates on aligning organizational goals with meaning and impact. While it shares attributes with transformational leadership, such as meaningful work and shared goals, purpose-driven leadership takes this a step further, prioritizing long-term societal impact, ethical decision-making with a commitment to sustainability.

Despite these qualities, neither fully captures the essence of inclusion.

That led me to the Inclusive Leadership Framework (ILC), a data-driven *behavioral* based model. Unlike one's attributes, which are often intrinsic characteristics, a behavior is extrinsic, learnable, actionable and measurable.

An attribute—such as charisma—may inspire but is not easily quantifiable or defined evenly across cultures. However, inclusive leadership centers on specific, measurable behaviors in which leaders can practice, refine and improve over time.

What sets the ILC model apart is its global application organisationally. Indeed, many if not all of the behaviours allow for greater innovation. That in turn creates a path to embed inclusion into everyday interactions and decision-making, an essential organisational component. The Inclusive leadership model is not a standalone and can be easily integrated into any leadership framework.

These behaviours shape how people experience inclusion in the workplace. Joseph Folkman and Jack Zenger write that inclusion is ultimately about perception. We may think we're inclusive, but how others experience us is what matters. Their research shows that inclusion and exclusion are not abstractions, but personal experiences felt by everyone.

For this reason, Chapter 2 begins with a real-life story on exclusion rather than a hazy definition on inclusion. Subsequent stories share experiences we've all felt. Each one is a real workplace scenario to show the impact of inclusion. The ideas presented are to get you to pause and think. It will hopefully provide clarity to build a place for fulfilling careers where employees can maximize their impact. We look at inclusion through a broader lens, seeing that it is not a solitary concept, but a holistic approach to leadership and how we choose to behave.

Why This Book? A Guide to Inclusive Leadership Through Coaching

This is a 'guidebook' with tools to develop inclusive leadership through coaching. By blending doctoral research, real-world stories and actionable points, it equips the reader to understand inclusion and apply it. There are reflective questions in every chapter to make inclusion both achievable and measurable, with the tools to lead inclusively.

We began our inclusion story in an outrigger canoe. Next is the experience of exclusion at work. Both inclusion and exclusion shape how one views the world and leads, how one behavior makes inclusion easier to adopt, while other behaviors require greater effort and commitment to develop.

We evaluate inclusion through real-life applications:

- In talent selection: A high-performing leader on the brink of losing her role and how a shift in listening makes all the difference.
- Mid-career coaching: Opportunities for coaching mid-career professionals at a global bank and tech firm, keeping each group engaged, embedding inclusion into the work environment.
- Dual-career couples: An oft-overlooked talent pool and the future of talent.
- In organizational change: How the ILC framework transformed Asia Pacific factory leaders and their teams.
- Now and in the future, the evolving impact of technology and inclusion, the ever-changing role of AI in development, coaching and building inclusion.

A Roadmap for Action

A note on confidentiality: Every story I've shared is based on my notes real experiences, events, and conversations, just the names and industries have been changed. Whether you are a coach, a leader, or an HR professional, you should find a story to help make inclusion part of your practice. Similar to the outrigger canoe paddling, inclusive leadership requires intentionality, alignment, and collective movement. Each chapter builds upon the last, with essential elements of inclusion, bringing together key reflections and questions for Coaching Inclusion in the final chapter.

A Flexible Approach for Readers

The book is to be used in a way that fits your needs. Whether insights on leadership behaviors, team dynamics or practical coaching strategies, each chapter has singular value while contributing to the big picture of inclusive leadership.

Chapter 2 explores exclusion and its impacts on business, why conviction matters in altering behaviors. Without conviction, change stays only at the surface.

Chapters 3–5 incorporate the Inclusive Leadership Compass, based on four areas: Self, Others, Teams, and Culture. It starts with Self-Awareness, how perception, intention, and impact shape leadership effectiveness, then to empathy as a leadership skill, helping leaders build trust and strengthen relationships within teams. Closing with humility, informal networks, and the role of perception management, essential for inclusive leadership.

Chapter 6 addresses the organizational roadblocks which hinder inclusion. We take a closer look at onboarding, talent management and evolving leadership models, reviewing outdated practices and new strategies for inclusive pathways.

Chapters 7 and 8 are career focused, an overlooked inclusion topic. The chapters touch upon mid-career and dual-career professionals and how organizations can better adapt career strategies for today's global talent challenge. We introduce the Intelligent Career Card System as a structured approach for dual-career couples to make informed and collaborative career decisions.

Chapter 9 is a how-to for building an inclusive culture, using a case study with factory leaders who created organizational change.

In Chapters 10 and 11 we bring in the executive perspective, what C-suite leaders really think about inclusion, coaching and the rise of AI-powered tools to facilitate both.

In Chapter 12, we pull it all together, compiling reflective questions and learning from each chapter. This structured yet flexible guide is designed to support ongoing practice and application of inclusive coaching.

The Bigger Picture: Inclusion as a Strategic Imperative

Each chapter assesses inclusive behaviors and strategies to embed inclusion, and a central theme emerges: Inclusion is not a policy or program. It recognizes unique strengths, stories and experiences each employee brings to the organization. The essence of inclusive leadership is not one person paddling harder, but to have everyone move in rhythm, in sync, creating momentum for changes that will endure.

Over 200 years ago, William Blake wrote: 'To see the world in a grain of sand.' Look at the whole person, which is to see greater potential and develop others in a rapidly changing world.

My sincere hope is that from this book you will see that inclusion is not as a 'nice-to-have' but is a necessary business imperative for the future of work.

Inclusion has a human side and a business side, both equally important, particularly when inclusion is missing.

Why Should You Practice Inclusion at Work?

I believe hitting financial targets and using inclusion metrics are commercially intertwined, interdependent, and indispensable. Research by Catalyst (2020), Google (2024), and Gartner, shows that inclusive workplaces show that inclusive workplaces produce better problem solving, higher engagement, faster business outcomes and more innovative dialogue.

Here's the rub: only 40% of employees think their managers actively promote inclusion (Rai and Dutkiewicz 2022). Yet that also means there is a large number of inclusive leaders who seek out different perspectives, encouraging debate or questioning decisions, even from those in power. Conversely, when teams feel excluded, they rate the inclusivity of their leadership much lower, hardly a surprise.

Inclusion as Strategy: What Drives Results and What Could Get in the Way

Why It Matters to Business Work environments are always changing influenced by demographic shifts, technology, and mobility. Inclusion is not just a value; it's a necessity for survival. Candidates are paying attention, too; many consider a company's commitment to inclusion when making career decisions. In a world where disruption is the norm, organizations that fail to embrace inclusion risk being left behind.

Why It Matters to People Companies prioritizing inclusion have an advantage in attracting talent. According to Deloitte (2023a, b), more than 80% of organizations reported DEI, purpose, sustainability, and trust as top focus areas in the 2023 Global Human Capital Trends survey. This represents a shift in expectations, with employees and candidates look for work environments that embrace difference and value connection. By creating environments where individuals feel valued for their contributions, companies are not only improving their cultures but also drive innovation and success.

Why It Matters in New Technologies There are two schools of thought here, particularly with AI-powered tools. Pauline Kim, (2017) Professor of Law at Washington University warns of "classification bias", or hiring algorithms designed to reduce bias unintentionally replicated structural inequities found in their training data. On the other hand, Orly Lobel, (2022) Warren Distinguished Professor of Law at the University of San

Diego and author of The Equality Machine, Harnessing Digital Technology for a Brighter, More Inclusive Future, argues that AI, when built with inclusive principles, actively promotes equity. Lobel suggests that AI has the ability to challenges rather than stereotypes rather particularly when organizations intentionally design algorithms to question assumptions and biases.

What's at Stake DEI is facing significant resistance, particularly in the United States repealing DEI programs in government and universities, placing federal DEI professionals on leave, signaling a dramatic policy shift. Major corporations are taking the same path with McDonald's, Meta, Target, Walmart, Amazon, and Berkshire Hathaway scaling back their DEI initiatives or removing DEI from their annual reports, setting a precedent that could impact global markets. This rollback threatens to stall progress on inclusion just as the need for diverse perspectives and talent has never been greater.

This resistance isn't isolated. According to TechTarget (2025), political and legal pressures are reshaping corporate diversity, equity, and inclusion (DEI) commitments. Confronted with a difficult choice, organizations either adapt to the pressure or remain committed to DEI initiatives. Some companies have bowed to external pressure, some have renamed and reframed their DEI functions, while others have continued to invest in these efforts. Inclusion remains a market-driven necessity, shaped by consumer expectations and the global competition for talent. This pushback threatens to derail progress at a time when organizations, governments, and communities should prioritize putting humanity back into the workplace, a shift best achieved through inclusive leadership.

It's easy to lose sight of what inclusion means.

At its core, inclusion is about connecting with others. This connection builds trust and engagement. Combining all three strengthens business and drives outcomes. In the next chapter, we'll look at what gets in the way of delivering outcomes: exclusion.

References

Catalyst. (2020, August 20). *Why diversity and inclusion matter: Quick take.* https://www.catalyst.org/insights/2020/why-diversity-and-inclusion-matter

Deloitte. (2023a). Asia Pacific Impact Report 2023: People. Retrieved from https://www.deloitte.com/au/en/about/governance/asia-pacific-impact-report-people.html

Deloitte. (2023b). *2023 Global human capital trends: New fundamentals for a boundaryless world.* https://www2.deloitte.com/us/en/insights/focus/human-capital-trends/2023/future-of-workforce-management.html

Google. (2024). *Diversity annual report 2024.* https://belonging.google/diversity-annual-report/2024/

Kim, P. T. (2017). Data-driven discrimination at work. *William & Mary Law Review, 58*(3), 857–936. https://scholarship.law.wm.edu/wmlr/vol58/iss3/3

Lobel, O. (2022). The equality machine: Harnessing digital technology for a brighter, more inclusive future. PublicAffairs.

Rai, T., & Dutkiewicz, C. (2022, May 10). *How to navigate pushback to diversity, equity and inclusion efforts.* Gartner. https://www.gartner.com/en/articles/how-to-navigate-pushback-to-diversity-equity-and-inclusion-efforts

TechTarget. (2025, February 27). *U.S. companies scale back DEI initiatives under new federal directive.* https://www.techtarget.com/searchhrsoftware/news/366568899/US-companies-scale-back-DEI-initiatives-under-new-federal-directive

CHAPTER 2

The Hidden Cost of Exclusion: The Silent Disruptor

The wound is the place where the light enters you.
Rumi

Sometimes a single experience can change your entire thinking. That's all it takes. Here's mine.

I was standing in front of a large corporate group in Singapore and asked their senior leaders to pair off and discuss what 'inclusion' meant to them, what it felt like.

It's a simple question. I've asked it many times across Asia and the Middle East. It's also a good way to discuss what the profile of an inclusive leader may look like. Everyone has experiences of inclusion, even if they don't call it inclusion, so it's always intriguing when I hear stories around that one simple word.

As I walked around the room, everyone was in earnest discussion. I saw the CEO had not paired up with anyone and overheard him say: 'we're talking about business now.' 'OK, so be it', I thought, 'this isn't his time to present' and let it go rather than redirect him.

After milling around, I asked the senior team to share their insights. I added that if anyone wanted to first add some preliminary thoughts please say so.

The CEO was the only one to raise his hand. "Yes. I need to say that we didn't answer your question" and almost smiled at me.

Taken aback a bit, I paused. But before I could reply, he continued. "Actually, we discussed *exclusion* instead."

'Oh', I thought, 'this is good,' and asked him to continue.

What followed was unexpected. As he was the CEO, the room fell silent, and all eyes were on him as he remained at his table. He turned his seat to face everyone and began to recount his own story of being excluded.

"I used to work for X and right after joining was asked to attend an executive committee meeting, an extended offsite in Bali. I remember clearly listening as the Chairman and others presented a buyout strategy. I'd heard some rumours about it but until then had no details."

"As I listened, I could see some gaps in their M&A plan. I didn't see it the same way they did, not even close. I'm a numbers person and coincidentally knew the financial weaknesses of the company they wanted to purchase, as I'd dealt with them before."

"So, as I listened, I looked around and assumed Finance and Legal would start poking some holes in the presentation. No one said a word. That was awkward."

"Well," I thought, "I am part of the executive committee now, they're paying me for my expertise, I know where the skeletons are buried [with this company] so might as well give them their money's worth. So I raised my hand."

"I know what you're aiming for here, but you may not know that I actually know [the other company] and used to deal with them. So I've got to tell you that if we go this way, there's the potential for a big hit, I honestly don't think it'll work to our advantage very much, sorry to say. And we could get battered reputationally. I can give you more details about them right now if you'd like."

The CEO paused for a minute. "I'm skipping the details of the presentation and the company, as it's not relevant, and this is actually the first time I've shared this publicly." He then continued his story.

"I wasn't sure if I should have jumped in like that, but felt they were going off track and no one was addressing the potential shortfall of this deal. So, when I spoke, I did so respectfully, I was careful about that."

"So, after a few seconds of silence-which seemed much longer the Chairman nodded my way and thanked me for my insights. The other committee members looked in different directions, but no one said a word! No one. The meeting ended with no change of direction."

"They spent the remainder of the offsite relaxing, enjoying the food, sunshine and fresh air. And would you believe it, there were closed-door meetings of which my team and I were excluded! They'd obviously decided to make the purchase, which they did. And yes, it turned out to be a financial hit."

He paused again, looked down at the floor for a minute, then said:

"Look, I have to honestly tell all of you that I'm really not certain what it means to be *inclusive*. But what I *can* tell you is that I was excluded. And I experienced the financial and reputational implications from being ignored and not included. And that's why we're having this conversation today."

Not easy for a CEO to be that open, and everyone seemed to be able to relate to his descriptions. With his story, the light entered the room, illuminating unspoken truths. The room almost leaned, a profound moment of quiet reflection. It certainly set an interesting tone for the rest of the day.

As that CEO had experienced, inclusion and profit are by no means separate.

"Inclusion" is vastly overused today and oft misunderstood. And yet... Inclusion is the catalyst that moves diversity and equity from concepts into practice, making certain that diverse perspectives are heard, considered, and integrated. Everyone knows the word but grapples with an easy definition. Let me give it some context and some [of my] definitions.

Inclusion is an enabler of outcomes; an inclusive business strategy can achieve better financial results. It should be woven into the organizational fabric from the processes, systems, activities, meetings, teamwork and, of course, from the leadership. Each factor is connected to inclusion, which cascades from the top down.

I've coached executives for over 25 years and heard many stories of exclusion, usually unintentional or unrecognized until it's called out-which is infrequent. Inclusion, however, gives a leader greater awareness, more cognizance of the intentions, the actions and reactions of others.

You may be reading this and think you're already aware of the above, that you're an evolved inclusive leader. But it's possible you have little idea how your actions and behaviours are interpreted by others.

Inclusive leadership centres on better understanding intent and impact. Traditional leadership emphasises self-reflection. Inclusive leadership adds an awareness of how your behaviour is experienced by others. In doing so, leaders should see that some of their well-intended actions might not be a positive experience for those involved.

Through my coaching practice, I've noticed patterns with inclusive leaders. Most exhibit common behaviours: a strong sense of self-awareness; recognizing biases in the moment and exceptional observation skills which allow them to learn from interactions and tactfully address non-inclusive behaviours. Being an inclusive leader requires:

- Acute Self-Awareness: Acknowledge those who make valuable contributions and know you're not the sole source of insight.
- Paying Attention: Undivided attention, no [immediate] judgment and allow a narrative to unfold without interrupting.
- Letting Others Lead: Let others take the lead, promote both autonomy and collective decision-making.
- Guiding diverse teams towards unity: facilitate constructive conversations and encourage healthy debate.
- Embedding Inclusion: Put inclusion into every aspect of the business so that it's integral to each part of the organization.

Has this always been the case? Over the past 25 years, I've observed a shift in how companies approach diversity and inclusion. While inclusive leadership has been a topic of academic research for two decades, its application in organizations is relatively recent, gaining traction over the past 10 years. Today, organizations recognize that inclusive leaders and cultures drive business performance and innovation. This shift is more common now than it was a decade ago, particularly in global companies that prioritize diverse markets and talent.

Leading inclusively is not a lofty ideal. It starts with a shift in behaviors placing more emphasis on listening over speaking, asking for different perspectives, and allowing others time to think and to encourage more open dialogue. It's paying attention when someone is excluded from a conversation or left off the talent plan. Inclusion can be learned and practiced by anyone open to flexing their leadership.

This is hardly a complete list.

My goal is not to provide 10 steps to inclusion. Inclusive leadership is a relatively new and evolving practice, approaching work and life with an open mind and continuous learning. A few years ago, Goldman Sachs launched an internal learning campaign called, 'Minds Wide Open,' a clever campaign that stuck with me. Those three words represented the essence of inclusion being open and willing to not only hear but also actively value and integrate ideas, particularly when they come from people or sources we might have overlooked. Inclusion goes beyond mere tolerance; it's about creating a space where every voice is genuinely considered and contributes to shared growth.

In any conversation, our minds wander, one comment or thought zigzags to another. Or we drift, filling the silence with small talk. Our brain is a vault of experiences, so when we chat the experiences signal the brain, triggering preferences, similarities and memories. All at once. With these 'data points' swirling around, are we really listening? Probably not as attentive as we should be.

In coaching executives, I found what sets many apart is their humility, empathy and listening skills, which interconnect and build on one another. Listening is tethered to empathy and humility by valuing others' perspectives while acknowledging our own limitations. Some may view humility as a weakness, others say they don't have enough time to listen. Listening is an immersion to understand what someone else is thinking. In doing so, we show humility, of not knowing all the answers. This listening approach is genuine interest in someone else's contributions and perspective. Every leadership book discusses the benefits of listening, but what I've noticed is more than simply listening; it is hearing with curiosity, no interruption or judgment.

Given the pace of change, inclusive leaders know their limitations and will step back to gather insights for better decision-making. Humility is vital to inclusion, knowing when to let others take the lead and coach (yes, coach) others towards success. While most leaders should have these basics, stress and tight deadlines can skew their strengths, which turns inclusion on its head.

When coaching I use the Thinking Environment, a listening technique developed by Nancy Kline, which encourages inclusive behaviours, respect, and psychological safety while minimizing power imbalances. I've used Kline's practice called listening pairs, a structured exercise where two individuals take turns speaking and listening without interruption or judgment, with a global bank in the Asia Pacific region as part of their diversity and talent management process. This simple yet powerful practice allowed participants to share their perspectives openly and reflect genuinely. The Managing Director of Corporate Banking was struck by the depth of these conversations and remarked, "I've never had conversations like these in my career. How did we manage to achieve this?" The answer lies in creating an environment that prioritizes genuine listening and empathy. It's nothing earth-shattering but requires a singular focus on inviting various perspectives and making space for authentic dialogue.

In contrast to the repetitive nature of "corporate-speak," where everyone seems to echo the same ideas, listening pairs cut through the noise. They help participants move beyond surface-level conversations and connect on a human level, enabling real insights and meaningful change.

We'll look into the Thinking Environment in subsequent chapters to show how this process supports inclusion, encourages dialogue, and bridges hierarchical divides. Under stress, inclusive practice can get sidelined. I often advise clients navigating stress on the need to pause and slow down.

In response I hear:

> I don't have time for this.
> I'm under pressure to get things done.
> I can't afford to wait for someone to respond.
> Honestly? Even if I suggest a 60 seconds pause, I've heard the same responses.

When I've led workshops on inclusion, I found that understanding inclusion often begins with reflecting on the impact of exclusion. Exclusion isn't just a theoretical concept it's something we've all experienced in different forms.

Opening a workshop with the question, "What does exclusion mean?" often unleashes a torrent of emotions. Studies by Dr. Naomi Eisenberger, Dr. Kipling D. Williams, and Dr. C. Nathan DeWall (2003) reveal that social exclusion activates brain regions associated with physical pain. But what about the exclusion we experience in today's workplace? For example, working intensely on a project might give us a sense of belonging, yet we may still feel disconnected from others. What does spending hours isolated in front of a laptop do to our ability to build relationships and connections?

We've all felt the sting of being ignored, dismissed, or overlooked. Even in the earlier story of the CEO, despite his position of privilege, he experienced acute exclusion, which became a turning point in his journey toward inclusive leadership. It is often in such moments that the true meaning of inclusion becomes clear.

Now you may be wondering: "This all makes sense, but can we really do this? Is it possible to create a work environment where everyone feels valued and genuinely included?" It might feel daunting, even idealistic, but it is achievable with the right mindset and tools. The simple answer is yes, of course you can and of course it can.

Reframe your perspective and start:

- Seeing each person through a lens of strengths, then decide if your perspective has altered at all.
- Spending time listening without interrupting, then decide whether it made any impact. Build your empathy and see how others react to you.
- If you followed those two points, do you think it would shift your leadership approach? By how much?

The questions are a starting point to see the organization through an inclusive filter. By adopting inclusive behaviours, leaders raise up others and add to the bottom line.

Inclusion isn't a check-the-box exercise on an organization's to-do list; it is a set of behaviors which increase personal and professional success, how you live, how you act, not merely how you show up to work.

You can't be 'inclusive' in a couple of days. It requires continuous effort, like going to the gym, strengthening your inclusive muscle through deliberate practice. I'm often asked a chafing question: 'are we supposed to prioritize inclusion more than our financial objectives? Is that more important?'

My reply: 'It's not 'either-or'; both carry equal weight.

The more relevant question is, 'how much more profitable can you become by embedding inclusion across the workforce?'

In the course of writing this book, most leaders I interviewed consider inclusion and effectiveness to be entwined into the firm's strategy, values, purpose and they bring an inclusive attitude into every interaction. Simply put, inclusivity brings both humanity and profit into the organization.

I've observed a stark contrast in the companies I advise. Some are still grappling with how to improve C-level diversity, while others are moving along steadily, having implemented inclusion strategies that seem to stick.

In conversations with C-suite executives, there's a clear recognition of the value of diverse perspectives to shape their business—from marketing, communications, R&D, finance, and policy to strategy, product innovation, and people decisions. Just as products are tailored for local tastes, it's now time to re-define leadership for the twenty-first century.

To do so, leaders need to draw on the strengths that diversity brings, using a behavioral rather than categorical approach. Leaders with conviction for inclusion will unlock opportunity. One important element is having conviction and 'walking the talk,' balancing between the evolution of work today and the imperative for inclusivity.

What Does Conviction Look Like?

Conviction in diversity and inclusion means prioritizing and articulating values, the fundamental step in building inclusive behaviors in the organization. When asked what it means to demonstrate conviction, I explain that it starts with understanding the company's DEI objectives and linking them to broader business goals. This understanding can lead to a reassessment of people management models, talent reviews, performance practices, and promotions. Leadership principles, vision, strategy, empowerment, and effective communication are powerful on their own and become more impactful when paired with inclusive behaviors.

To show conviction is to act; it begins by asking questions that challenge your thinking:

- *Do my actions show that diversity and inclusion are fundamental to our work?*
- *Is the management showing any more tolerance of others, or greater willingness to simply listen?*
- *Am I really creating an environment where we can see people feeling more encouraged and empowered to contribute?*
- *Am I 'coaching' others on inclusion or keeping it to myself?*

The goal is to create a workplace where diversity is seamlessly integrated, inclusion becomes second nature and prioritized not only for organizational success but also as a contribution to society. Takeda and LEGO demonstrate the role inclusion plays addressing societal needs and serving the community, defining business success through a commercial strategy and social impact. Takeda advances global health equity through access-to-medicine initiatives and local partnerships and was among the first companies to sign the World Economic Forum's *Zero Health Gap Pledge* (World Economic Forum 2023). LEGO has committed to using sustainable materials across all products by 2030, as part of its broader investment in environmental responsibility (LEGO Group 2020). These actions reflect how inclusion can extend beyond the workplace to strengthen community connection and contribute to long-term societal and business resilience.

As Beal et al. (2023) argue, financial institutions and by extension, other sectors can grow their business while tackling pressing issues such as financial inclusion, human rights, and climate justice. Their research highlights how the integration of social impact with business goals is not only possible but profitable.

Great Place to Work (2023) also found a strong link between social impact and business success. Over 100 organizations across industries, including technology, hospitality, retail, and financial services, have been recognized for putting their communities and employees first. These companies show that social impact is not only the right thing to do but also drives innovation and business growth. It makes sense: when employees feel valued and included, they build stronger connections and, in turn, drive better results.

It's as simple and as difficult as that.

The goal is to make inclusion a habit, part of the everyday, shaping how employees address and identify both problems and opportunities to design solutions. This inclusiveness gives both public and private sectors the option to rethink work, who does it, and where it gets done.

Throughout this book we explore a mix of real-life inclusive work examples and research-based strategies, you'll understand the practical approaches to various situations.

Before moving to the next chapter, think about your own leadership style and corporate culture with these three questions:

1. *What inclusive practices do you want most for your organization?*
2. *How might these improve your work, day-to-day, your team's and the business overall?*
3. *Would the impact of these changes be noticeable? If so, where within the business?*

In the next chapter, we examine some of the behaviours outlined in the Inclusive Leadership Compass and the benefits of leading inclusively. Through a case study, we focus on two areas: conviction and self-awareness, complemented by coaching questions designed to uncover the essence of inclusive leadership. Workplace scenarios further illustrate how to lead inclusively, grounded in the foundational principles of the Compass. Returning to Rumi's idea, we begin where awareness opens, and insight begins to emerge.

REFERENCES

Beal, D., Benayad, A., & Newsom Reeves, K. (2023, October 16). *Banks can deliver both social impact and profits. Here's how.* Boston Consulting Group. https://www.bcg.com/publications/2023/balancing-social-impact-and-profits-with-banking

Great Place to Work. (2023, August 31). *Companies that care 2023.* https://www.greatplacetowork.com/companies-that-care

LEGO Group. (2020, June 15). *The LEGO Group to invest up to US$400 million over three years to accelerate sustainability efforts.* https://www.lego.com/en-us/aboutus/news/2020/june/sustainability-investment

World Economic Forum. (2023). *Zero Health Gap Pledge: Global Health Equity Network.* https://initiatives.weforum.org/global-health-equity-network/pledge

PART II

Building Inclusive Leadership

CHAPTER 3

The Inclusive Leadership Compass Framework

Waking up to who you are requires letting go of who you imagine yourself to be.
Alan Watts

Organizations begin their DEI efforts with Unconscious Bias training. A great starting point, although it's being pilloried daily, and some companies are washing their hands of it. Which is silly, as biases need to be better understood and managed rather than eliminated. It should not be up for debate.

I went back to school for a doctorate years ago because I had noticed too many talented, highly educated women—and particularly Asian talent—being passed over for promotions despite consistently delivering results. I couldn't figure out why this was happening and felt we could do better. I decided to study leadership education and learn directly from women leaders in the Asia Pacific Region their leadership styles and the stories behind how they advanced their careers. During my research, I realized I wasn't as enlightened as I'd thought; my own biases surfaced quickly. Even with my cross-cultural experience, I'd applied cultural frameworks too rigidly, slotting others into a confined cultural box instead of seeing the whole person. Here I was, replicating the same exact behaviour I'd observed in countless multinational succession planning meetings.

With my cross-cultural experience, I had studied the research of Fons Trompenaars and Charles Hampden-Turner, as well as Erin Meyer, and applied these cultural frameworks too rigidly unintentionally slotting others into a confined cultural box rather than seeing the whole person. Their frameworks offer valuable insights into how culture shapes behavior, but I approached them too prescriptively.

For example, when I asked a leader in Japan a generic question about values, their response didn't fit with what I expected based on cultural dimensions. Rather than considering the individual's perspective, I rephrased the question in an attempt to elicit the answer I anticipated. Or worse, I discounted their response altogether. My lightbulb moment when I realized I was replicating the same behavior I had observed in countless multinational succession planning meetings. Inclusion requires moving beyond categories and labels.

I've facilitated unconscious bias workshops in Asia Pacific and the Middle East with organizations like Boeing, Eli Lilly, Morgan Stanley, Rockwell, Twitter, UBS, Visa, and multilateral institutions. I've seen how bias undermines DEI initiatives, often because of a misplaced reliance on Western models when deciding on career promotions. Over time, I started to see how leadership frameworks applied too rigidly were holding talented individuals back, especially in diverse cultural contexts. Although there's been some progress, workshops alone won't move the diversity needle. Inevitably participants in these workshops circle back weeks later and ask, "Now that I know what I know, what should I do?" This underscores the challenge of making learning stick.

One of the biggest obstacles I've found with such training is the failure to put into action the agreed commitments expressed in the workshop. The Guardian has written that despite 81% of companies implementing unconscious bias training, there's been a decrease in corporate confidence regarding its effectiveness.

To balance this skepticism, Daniel Kahneman and Amos Tversky's groundbreaking 1974 study on heuristics in Judgment under Uncertainty remains relevant today. Their research identified cognitive biases such as availability bias (the tendency to rely on readily available information) and anchoring bias (the tendency to rely heavily on the first piece of information encountered when making decisions). This work set the stage for extensive research into unconscious bias and its impact on decision-making, diversity, equity, and inclusion (DEI).

Kahneman's book Thinking, Fast and Slow became a landmark resource for understanding how biases influence behavior and how to mitigate their effects. Building on this foundation, entrepreneur Buster

Benson (2016) streamlined over 200 documented cognitive biases into a detailed visual representation of 150 biases, used with permission from John Manoogian III and Buster Benson, illustrating the complexity of human decision-making.

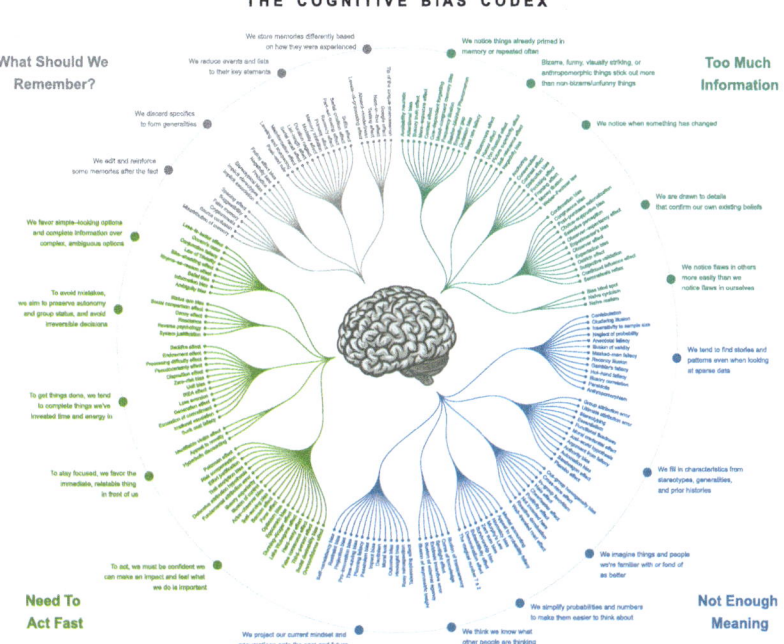

Originally published in 2016, this visual has been downloaded millions of times and widely reviewed on platforms like Medium. I often use Benson's visual in workshops to emphasize the enormity of cognitive biases. It serves as a starting point for an essential question: *with all this knowledge about bias, are we taking meaningful steps toward true inclusion?* Understanding bias is important, but it's only the first step. And typically, where most people stop. Inclusion requires action beyond awareness embedding inclusive behaviors and practices into every aspect of organizational culture. Biases have value and recognizing them is the first step of the process. My workshops slice through the complexities of diversity to show what we're unsure about ourselves, enabling some healthy soul-searching.

Kahneman reminds us of our inherent irrationality; no matter how much we believe we know about bias, we're all prone to confirmation bias. We start with biases then find reasons to justify them rather than forming impartial beliefs based on what we actually experience. To rid oneself of bias doesn't make sense and is impossible anyhow. Among 150 biases identified, similarity bias is the most egregious. It's the tendency to prefer those like us. It's common in hiring, task delegation, and promotions. Even with ongoing bias training, similarity bias is hard to eliminate.

But here's one approach I've used many times. In a short activity during a workshop, I ask participants to pair up with someone they know casually but not well (typical in the workplace). In 1–2 minutes, they have to find out what they have in common. Call it non-obvious similarities.

This short exercise connects on an emotional level, as it provides a brief yet valuable glimpse into the other person's life beyond their role or function, a starting point for relationship building. What's fascinating about this exercise is that people who think they know someone often realize they don't. And the reverse is true as well, which is the point.

For example, in one session, two participants who had never spoken before discovered they had grown up in the same small town in the Philippines. In another, two colleagues from Malaysia who worked at the company for more than 20 years, thought they had much in common and realized they were complete opposites when it came to food preferences, travel destinations, and even book choices. These quick conversations making small connections shift the way people relate to each other in the workshop and beyond.

Bias training has, over the past decade, vastly overshadowed the critical part of behaviors and actions that confront bias and build inclusion. And I understand why, working on inclusion requires self-reflection and this is the hard part. The good news is some of my clients are interested in bridging this awareness gap, looking for practical steps to facilitate inclusivity and reduce decision-making bias. What really counts, in both life and work, are the actions we choose beyond mere thought or biases.

WHAT ARE THOSE BEHAVIOURS?

A few years ago, while facilitating discussions on leadership and diversity, a client asked whether I had any assessments to develop an inclusive leader. I didn't.

Was there such a tool? I looked, and eventually found Dr. Sandy Sable and her business partner, Bernadette Dillon (2016), co-CEOs of the Inclusive Leadership Compass (ILC). They had the answer. I now use both the ILC Self and 360 Assessments.

There are many assessments on the market, with more appearing each month. I'd previously used the Hogan Leadership Series, a personality assessment. The Hogan Development Survey highlights patterns that might be problematic or become obstacles when someone is under stress. It also shows how interpersonal sensitivity, insightfulness, attentive listening, perceptiveness, understanding, and altruism all play important roles in inclusion.

While Hogan helped me understand how a leader's personality can shape the team environment, my client was looking for something more specific, an assessment designed to identify and develop inclusive leadership through observable behaviours, and to support a more inclusive organisation. The ILC focuses on what we do and why we do it, offering a behavioural lens that's essential for evaluating inclusive leadership and its impact.

INCLUSIVE BEHAVIOURS: A CORNERSTONE OF INCLUSIVE LEADERSHIP

The Inclusive Leadership Compass analyses behaviours across Self, Others, Team and Organisation. Like Hogan, it addresses strengths but identifies more behavioural strengths and points out developmental areas.

Inclusive Leadership Compass Framework

Dimension	Focus Area	Definition
Self	Conviction	Treats inclusion as a personal priority
Self	Openness	Actively seeks out different perspectives
Self	Self-awareness	Has a strong understanding of themselves and their impact on others
Self	Humility	Acknowledges personal limitations and mistakes
Others	Respect	Treats people with respect
Others	Fairness	Behaves fairly
Others	Personalization	Cares about people as individuals
Others	Participation	Encourages autonomy and involvement in decision-making
Team	Unity	Fosters cohesion within their team
Team	Facilitation	Facilitates the constructive exchange of different views and ideas
Team	Psychological safety	Creates an environment where people feel safe to speak up with ideas, questions, concerns, or mistakes
Team	Coaching	Actively develops the inclusive capability of team members
Organization	Vision & strategy	Aligns inclusion with the organization's strategy and values
Organization	Accountability	Promotes accountability for inclusion outcomes
Organization	Systems & processes	Integrates inclusion into employee practices
Organization	Work flexibility	Actively drives a flexible work culture

© Inclusive Leadership Compass

Inclusive Leadership Compass: Defining Focus Areas

Like other leadership models, Inclusive Leadership starts with self-awareness. What sets it apart is its pragmatic approach to identifying changeable behaviours coupled with data-informed steps for actions. After an ILC debrief, people won't ask, 'so now what am I supposed to do?" There's no ambiguity about next steps. They'll know how to apply it.

One of the fascinating aspects of inclusive leadership is the distinction between intention and impact. None of us go to work to exclude anyone. Yet we may react differently to stress or deadlines and excluding others can be an unfortunate by-product. Relying on an intent to be inclusive does not offer a complete picture of inclusion. As mentioned earlier, Drs. Jack Zenger and Joseph Folkman arrived at the same conclusion when researching leaders. *"Inclusivity is particularly in the eye of the beholder. You might intend to be inclusive, and even think you are inclusive, but your impact on others might be very different" (2017).*

Their study involved over 1.5 million raters and 122,000 leaders. It investigated leaders' efforts to include diverse perspectives and build an environment of trust and appreciation for differences. Their findings showed a large disconnect between how leaders perceive their own effectiveness in valuing diversity and how they were actually rated by a diverse, external group. A common pattern emerged. Leaders who were not necessarily best at inclusion overestimated their strengths in this area.

We've seen this with other leadership competencies, where some leaders remain blind to their shortcomings while others fail to acknowledge their strengths. Zenger and Folkman's work highlights the importance of external feedback in assessing inclusivity efforts. As self-perception is skewed, inclusion's true measure is its impact on others. Then closing this gap is key to building an inclusive company.

INCLUSIVE BEHAVIOUR: AN ESSENTIAL TOOL FOR INCLUSIVE LEADERSHIP

Equally important is measuring results. When advising clients or facilitating workshops, I often hear, "Inclusion is a nice-to-have, but we can't measure it." This mindset highlights a common misconception: the challenge is not that inclusion can't be measured, but that organizations often rely solely on raising awareness of inclusive concepts or focus only on unconscious bias without translating these into measurable behaviors and outcomes. To realize its benefits and assess its impact, organizations must adopt a clear set of inclusive leadership behaviors, such as those outlined in the Inclusive Leadership Compass, then assess culture, systems, and processes against those behaviors, linking them to tangible business results.

Research strongly supports the value of inclusion. One study found that organizations implementing inclusion initiatives reported a 70%

improvement in employees' sense of belonging and psychological safety, along with measurable gains in team performance, decision-making quality, and collaboration (Zheng et al. 2023). Similarly, research by Lorenzo et al. (2018) found that companies with above-average diversity in their management teams achieved 19% higher innovation revenue compared to those with below-average diversity, with 45% of total revenue attributed to the innovative contributions of diverse leadership strategies.

Through my experience using the ILC assessments and in coaching, I know all too well that any behavioural change requires time, intention, and effort. Is it easy to identify future leaders within a company? Easy to propose, harder to confirm. What I've found is that when leaders take time to reflect, they often realize that their long-held totems may actually be the stumbling blocks to achieving inclusivity. My coaching approach integrates data-driven evaluations and the Thinking Environment framework to assess inclusive behaviours and establish a reliable process to support real change.

EXAMINING SELF-AWARENESS AND CONVICTION

It starts with Self-Awareness. Conviction is when leaders look in the mirror and ask, *who do I want to be?* That's not a cliché. Such introspection is neither straightforward nor simple. It requires a shift in thinking and observation.

Self-awareness may well be a starting point in every leadership model, but few take the time to grapple with it, as they're either in a senior role or too busy or scared to reflect. A typical coachee takes on a new job. It demands their full attention; they're not focused on themselves or the world around them. They jump right into the role until they see that something gives them pause. It could be external feedback, overheard complaints, hallway gossip, nudges or silent that tell the coaches something's not clicking.

But not all leaders are attuned to such signals.

Through a structured reflection process (not merely navel gazing) you can see the patterns of what you do or overlook and forget to do. Acknowledging such patterns builds strength and humility. Not easy, but ignoring this step overlooks the essence of reflective leadership development. I remember during an inclusion workshop one participant asked if we could just skip the 'self-reflection' part, as he felt it would be too awkward. Not an uncommon request, either.

Without self-reflection and real-time feedback, leaders fall back on familiar strengths, such as prioritizing productivity or pursuing excellence. Both are noble goals, but *over*-emphasizing might derail the work. Clinging to a few strengths can diminish other leadership behaviours.

A relevant example was that of Brynna, one of my coaching clients, an exceptionally bright leader with global potential with a FMCG multinational. Originally from Poland with extensive experience in the UK and the USA, Brynna moved to Bangkok to lead their design team. Her team grew from 5 to 25 members across Asia in 3 years, broadening her role. She then relocated to Singapore and was leading her former peers in China, India, Indonesia, Japan, Malaysia, and Vietnam.

When I asked her who she wanted to be as a leader, she responded, 'I want to be recognized as a fair leader dedicated to developing my team. And then added, 'inclusion is not only a strength but my personal commitment.'

When I interviewed her stakeholders, I added questions of inclusivity and team dynamics. The feedback was mixed regarding her inclusiveness. Her boss in New Jersey and her main sponsor in San Francisco had concerns about Brynna's cross-cultural awareness specifically her blunt communication style. Her team in Asia thought she had some clear cultural sensitivity, but more than half pointed out instances of exclusion and favouritism. Although she'd said inclusivity was key to her leadership, the feedback said it wasn't, echoing Folkman and Zenger's disconnect between intention and impact.

Conviction? Not Just Yet

When I gave Brynna the feedback, she had a hard time hearing it, much less accepting such comments. She truly saw herself as an inclusive leader, convinced she'd made her team feel included and valued. Those who'd felt excluded had pointed comments. "In meetings, if someone gives a wrong answer, Brynna moves to interrogation mode. We joke about 'how wise (why's) she is', such as:

- Why it didn't work?
- Why were the numbers wrong?
- Why the project is off-track?
- And more why's.

She was unaware that her inquisitive style and questioning created an atmosphere of fear.

Another mentioned "there's a division here, those in Brynna's inner circle and the rest of us." This perceived favouritism led to an environment where tasks were funnelled through a select group, detracting from the team's business focus.

Her strength was being inquisitive, a quick thinker with a proclivity for problem solving. Those strengths also resulted in over preparation by her direct reports whenever there was a meeting. "I over-prepare my team with a list of 100 potential questions that Brynna might ask so they do well at her meetings."

Others compared working with Brynna to living in a pressure cooker, where meetings felt like high-stakes cross-examinations. While a few appreciated Brynna's style, saying her questioning kept them on their toes, many also described it as relentless.

After the debrief session, Brynna recognized the need to take a step back and reflect on how her actions supported her stated goal and personal priority of being an inclusive leader. This would have been a completely different coaching engagement if she hadn't been willing to reflect.

I asked, how she might be perceived by her team and whether her leadership style demonstrated equal treatment with everyone? This reflection required her to examine her patterns and consider what changes she needed to make her leadership more consistent with her values and priorities.

Brynna, like many leaders, tended to make quick judgments about people but had a talent for recruiting strong performers. But she struggled with patience for those who couldn't keep up with her rapid pace or who were unprepared to answer her pointed questions. She addressed these challenges by implementing individual performance improvement plans.

While these plans aimed to boost team performance, they inadvertently reinforced similarity bias, within months, her core team began to resemble her. This created a dynamic where idea exchanges and debates became an echo chamber. Her questioning style, though still pointed, was perceived as more tolerable by those who aligned with her.

This also led to a second unintended consequence: favouritism as Brynna relied heavily on her "go-to" employees, the ones who mirrored her style and always delivered under the pressure of tight deadlines.

Creating a toxic cycle that sidelined others, categorizing this group as "needs development."

Exclusion can be papered over as 'needs development', and staying in that category adds to disengagement or redundancies. Perceptions settle into corporate murmurs, making it harder for others to even be considered for different roles with 'reputation' bias. Assigning projects to the same people because they always deliver and assuming others lack the necessary skills can only stunt their growth. If you rely on your fastest horse to win all the time, the horse collapses.

Brynna didn't want to be seen as exclusive or treating people unfairly. Her narrow focus on results, relying on the same go-to person, especially under pressure impacted her leadership effectiveness. This is where coaching helped, serving as a trusted, non-judgmental, sounding board to refine behaviours and try new approaches.

In Brynna's case, we began with four key questions designed to surface blind spots, both areas of hesitation and overused strengths, and sharpen her awareness of how her leadership was landing with others.

Self-Awareness Coaching Questions As we worked through the Stakeholder Feedback and the Hogan Leadership Series, we examined Brynna's inclusive strengths and verbatim comments before moving on to developmental areas. One theme emerged: inquisitiveness, when overused, especially in combination with boldness and skepticism, had the potential to derail her goal of being viewed as an inclusive leader. The Hogan profile, which identifies leadership strengths and derailers under stress, flagged these traits as potential risks. Stakeholder interviews corroborated this, Brynna's inquisitive nature was often perceived as questioning others' motives and intentions. Additionally, when responses seemed ill-prepared, she tended to distrust the individuals entirely.

I started with four questions to help Brynna reshape her own perceptions and how others see her.

1. **Who do you want to become?** This question gets to the heart of understanding oneself and the kind of leader one aspires to be. It's a simple question to ask but a complex one to answer and yet, it is essential to begin any meaningful change. For Brynna, this question prompted a moment of reflection: *"I want to be seen as a leader who inspires trust and respect while driving results. I believe in pushing*

my team to achieve their best, but I also want to be someone they feel supported by."

My Interpretation: Brynna's response reflected her aspiration to balance high expectations with a more supportive leadership style. To help her examine this further, I encouraged her to look back on pivotal events that shaped who she is as a leader and connect her values to those moments. Values guide how leaders make decisions and shape team culture. Reconnecting with her values and defining what she wanted to accomplish became a starting point for change.

2. **How does your leadership style intersect with the behavior of inclusivity?** Can you say that your leadership promotes inclusion? When asked, Brynna admitted: *"I'm direct, and I believe in keeping people accountable. But I sometimes feel that my style might come across as too sharp or demanding."*

    My Interpretation: This candid admission revealed Brynna's awareness of the tension between her results-driven approach and her desire to create an inclusive environment. Her style, while effective for accountability, risked alienating team members who needed her to acknowledge their strengths.

    We focused on promoting inclusivity by recognizing each team member's strengths and tailoring feedback to motivate and engage them. I suggested she use Marshall Goldsmith's 4C method and reflect on whether a comment *'will help the person I'm talking to.' If the answer is no, then it's better left unsaid.* (p. 69). I also recommended offering five words of genuine appreciation before delivering constructive feedback. Admittedly, this suggestion often meets with resistance.

    Clients frequently ask: *"Do I need to come up with exactly five words?" "Would two be enough?" "Is it okay to just say they're hardworking?"*

    True appreciation focuses on a person's character strengths, such as curiosity, empathy, or resilience, rather than simply praising their work ethic. Expressing appreciation changes the conversation. Research by Marcial Losada and Emily Heaphy, John Gottman, Nancy Kline, and Shelly Gable underscores that positive reinforcement has a measurable impact on team dynamics, relationships, and performance (Gable et al. 2004; Gottman 1994; Kline 2023; Losada and Heaphy 2004).

Brynna asked the same questions. The answer lies in the intention behind the words to authentically highlight a person's strengths before addressing areas for improvement. While this feedback method may feel awkward, it shifts the dynamic from criticism to collaboration. Promoting inclusivity required Brynna to acknowledge the strengths of each team member and tailoring her feedback to motivate them.

3. **What obstacles might hinder your progress toward becoming an inclusive leader?**

    When asked about potential obstacles, Brynna shared: *"I think my impatience will be a hurdle. I struggle when people don't meet my expectations like not coming to a meeting prepared and not offer a cogent response. I also get frustrated when they can't keep up with the pace I set."*

    My Interpretation: Brynna's recognition of impatience as a barrier provided a starting point for our work. We discussed how her impatience might inadvertently exclude other perspectives and ultimately impact inclusivity. Through our discussion, Brynna considered steps to balance high expectations and openness to different communication styles and contributions.

    What constitutes a strength in one cultural setting may be a liability in another. Even the pursuit of excellence has its limitations. Her strengths as a direct communicator and her curiosity, while powerful, when paired with her emphasis on excellence and results, undermined instead of enhancing team unity. To help her navigate this challenge, I guided Brynna to shift her reliance on a select few "go-to" employees to recognize how strengths in others for better collective outcome. Over time, she reversed similarity bias by finding commonalities in team members she previously overlooked. This shift moved from favoritism to a more impartial approach creating a starting point for inclusive leadership.

4. **What support do you need to become a more inclusive leader?**

    When asked Brynna said: *"I need help understanding how to balance my drive for results with creating a space where my team feels they can contribute freely."*

    My Analysis: This insight led us to focus on strategies to help Brynna build trust and inclusivity without compromising on performance.

My Approach: To address this, I suggested ways to evaluate and balance her approach. This began with paying attention to her gut reactions—her triggers—and pausing to reflect before acting. I also recommended ending each day with four questions:

- *Could I have approached any of these situations differently?*
- *How did my actions affect others emotionally?*
- *Were there highs and lows today? What was their impact on me and others?*

From this practice, Brynna had a better sense of her impact and actions needed to be inclusive.

Inclusive Leadership and Self-Awareness

Inclusive leadership begins with acute self-awareness, which, in this coaching engagement, led to greater awareness of Brynna's impact on others. But genuine self-reflection is rare, as we deceive ourselves into believing we are self-aware when we are not. Tasha Eurich, PhD, found that while many believe they possess self-awareness, only a small fraction really do.

Brynna's experience mirrored this reality. While the stakeholder feedback served as a wake-up call, seeing herself through the eyes of others was neither immediate nor easy. She thought she was inclusive, but her team and other colleagues had a different experience. Letting go of that imagined self, took effort and practice. She wasn't dismissive. At first, she justified her actions. Shifting her approach wasn't immediate either. She welcomed the feedback, particularly when it came to her inquisitive style, which is often hard to let go of a strength. Over time, she began to realize the gap between intention and impact and gradually adjusted her approach.

One area we worked on was how she framed questions. Brynna often used the "Five Whys" method, assuming it would lead to better problem-solving. But her instinct to lead with 'why' unintentionally created a blame-oriented culture, where pointing fingers became the norm a dynamic her team felt daily. I've observed other leaders do the same, not recognize the impact repeated 'why' questions can have on team morale.

Shifting to 'what' questions helped Brynna open up dialogue and create an environment for co-creating solutions. Asking, *"What might we be missing?"* or *"What else should we consider?"* created a different tone and direction. But this shift wasn't only about changing her language, it was about reshaping how she saw herself as a leader. In the process, she did the difficult but necessary work of releasing who she imagined herself to be, making space for who she could become.

In the next chapter, you'll uncover insights on empathy and how self-awareness serves as a foundational first step. Through introspective questions, you'll be encouraged to reflect on the type of leader you aspire to be. Looking back at the end of the day not only strengthens self-awareness but also stretches empathy, helping you bridge the gap between intention and impact in your inclusive leadership journey.

References

Benson, B. (2016, September 1). *Cognitive bias cheat sheet: 4 conundrums of intelligence.* Medium. https://medium.com/thinking-is-hard/4-conundrums-of-intelligence-2ab78d90740f

Dillon, B., & Sable, S. (2016). Inclusive Leadership Framework. Retrieved from https://www.organizationwebsite.com/framework

Gable, S. L., Reis, H. T., Impett, E. A., & Asher, E. R. (2004). *What do you do when things go right? The intrapersonal and interpersonal benefits of sharing positive events.* Journal of Personality and Social Psychology, 87(2), 228–245. https://doi.org/10.1037/0022-3514.87.2.228

Gottman, J. M. (1994). *Why marriages succeed or fail: And how you can make yours last.* Simon & Schuster.

Kahneman, D., & Tversky, A. (1974). Judgment under uncertainty: Heuristics and biases. Science, 185(4157), 1124–1131. https://doi.org/10.1126/science.185.4157.1124

Kline, N. (2023). *I Promise Not to Interrupt: Building Thinking Environments for Real Conversations.* Penguin Business.

Lorenzo, R., Voigt, N., Tsusaka, M., Krentz, M., & Abouzahr, K. (2018, January 23). *How diverse leadership teams boost innovation.* Boston Consulting Group. https://www.bcg.com/publications/2018/how-diverse-leadership-teams-boost-innovation

Losada, M., & Heaphy, E. (2004). The Role of Positivity and Connectivity in the Performance of Business Teams: A Nonlinear Dynamics Model. American Behavioral Scientist, 47(6), 740–765. https://doi.org/10.1177/0002764203260208

Zheng, W., Kim, J., Kark, R., & Mascolo, L. (2023, September 27). *What makes an inclusive leader.* Harvard Business Review. https://hbr.org/2023/09/what-makes-an-inclusive-leader

CHAPTER 4

Empathy in Action Leading Inclusive Teams

Empathy is the connective tissue of a functional society.
Jamil Zaki

As we saw with Brynna, none of us intend to exclude others, but work constraints can lead to narrowing our circles, dialing back discussions and deferring to familiar, go-to team members. We don't realize the slippery slope of overusing strengths, favouring efficiency over inclusivity, leaning on a few rather than the whole team. It takes a wake-up call, like high turnover on a team, to see the cost of our preferences.

THE DECLINE AND REVIVAL OF EMPATHY

Empathy is the core of humanity. It is our moral compass that guides inclusion. Yet over the decades there's been a decline in empathy. In the U.S., a study of 14,000 college students between 1979 and 2009 reported a decrease in empathy, with a significant drop occurring after 2000. More recently, however, research suggests a potential reversal of this trend. A 2024 study found an increase in empathic traits among younger generations in the U.S. after 2008, hinting that we may see more empathetic leaders emerging in the next generation. Studies in Asia have examined empathy with mixed results, often influenced by cultural norms and societal expectations. Some research highlights differences in how empathy is expressed across professional roles or cultural contexts, emphasizing the complexity of studying empathy within the region.

I've found two areas of coaching for inclusion, one where a leader is viewed as overusing empathy and the other where a leader is viewed as lacking empathy. With a tailored approach both can be addressed. For the highly empathic leaders, the focus is often on creating boundaries and learning how to balance empathy with objectivity. For leaders struggling with low empathy, the focus is on self-awareness and perspective taking to connect with others. In both cases, empathy, when practiced, can become the superpower that transforms teams.

As a leader, your team wants someone they can rely on, someone who balances the demands of work with their well-being. This is where empathy steps in, not just being open to different viewpoints but also connecting with the emotions and experiences behind them. Many of my coaching clients struggle with authenticity while trying to show empathy. For example, the head of digital marketing for a global finance company in Hong Kong told me, "I've gotten feedback from everyone that I need to be more empathetic. OK, but am I supposed to change who I am completely? It's not me; it's that I feel awkward repeatedly asking my team, 'So, how are you feeling?'"

The Science of Empathy

Empathy is not a fixed trait; it's a skill that leaders can develop through intentional effort. Jamil Zaki, in his book *The War for Kindness: Building Empathy in a Fractured World*, describes empathy as a mental superpower. He outlines two key components: emotional empathy (feeling another's experience) and cognitive empathy (understanding their perspective). Leaders who develop both create environments where their teams feel valued and heard. It's not about repeatedly asking, "How are you feeling?" but about forming genuine connections.

Roman Krznaric's (2014) book, *Empathy: Why It Matters and How to Get It*, introduces six habits of highly empathic people:

1. Switch on Your Empathic Brain
2. Make the Imaginative Leap
3. Seek Experiential Adventure
4. Practice the Craft of Conversation

5. Travel in Your Armchair (transport yourself into other people's minds)
6. Inspire a Revolution

Neuroscience shows that empathy activates areas of the brain linked to decision-making and collaboration which are fundamental for inclusive leadership. These insights highlight the importance of blending emotional and cognitive empathy to shape a team culture of trust and respect.

William's Story: Bridging an Empathy Deficit

Working for a global consumer products company in Hong Kong, we were searching for a finance and tax expert which led us to find William. A native of Hong Kong, he had an impressive resume, solid experience, education, a robust financial career, and was an engaging conversationalist who captivated everyone. His combination of professional acumen, excellent communication skills and a comprehensive understanding of finance and tax made him a compelling candidate. He navigated through the interview process with ease, leaving a lasting impression of optimism and high expectations among the interview panel.

The final and perfunctory step was the reference checks, which I was tasked to complete. Typically straightforward, the feedback on him was unexpectedly critical and harsh, casting doubt over his candidacy. I flagged it with the hiring manager as a flashpoint and to slow things down. However, the urgency to fill the position led our Senior Vice President to proceed with the hire, overlooking potential red flags I'd advised him on.

William's work may have been impeccable, but it was also clear that his former colleagues did not appreciate his management style.

William joined as the VP. And, yes, his financial reporting was flawless, but you wouldn't call him a leader who inspired others. There was a visible lack of team cohesion. During the annual budget, he and his team worked around the clock until final approval was obtained, which often took months. Everyone knew the budgeting process was broken and there were some half-hearted attempts to reduce the team's workload, it never seemed to happen.

The company was shifting towards building an inclusive culture with a focus on well-being, William found this shift challenging. As the workload increased, he doubled downed on becoming more directive, telling the team they were on call 24/7 if needed. William's approach to the budgeting process felt more like a constraint than an opportunity to the employees.

He was adamant that there be no mistakes which is next to impossible in budgeting and his over-control evolved into bureaucratic checklists, a command-and-control style that was unsustainable.

The tipping point came with the arrival of a new boss. Although I was the head of talent for a different division, his boss asked me to be William's coach to help him stay focused on the outcomes. William participated in a 360 Emotional Intelligence assessment and received feedback from 18 stakeholders, which was unvarnished and eye-opening.

Some of the feedback described him as:

- Believing he was smarter than everyone else.
- A workaholic who expects the same level of commitment from his team.
- Impulsive, overly direct, obsesses over minor mistakes.
- Narrowly focused on details, loses sight of the bigger picture and the team.
- Lacking listening skills and overly hands-on.
- Technically proficient but not good with interpersonal relationships.

The Coaching Process

The feedback shocked William. He'd been promoted and rewarded throughout his career, leading him to assume he was doing everything right. His response? "After all this time, they just don't understand me." He was taken aback and asked if I could be a sounding board to help him process the feedback. He vented, and I listened. To him, the feedback made no sense. He had been consistently promoted and rewarded and assumed he was on the right path.

The truth is this feedback wasn't new; it had been shared with his previous boss. William's intense focus on outcomes often overshadowed concerns about his perceived lack of approachability. It's a dynamic I've observed in organizations: when someone delivers results, their behavior, no matter how disruptive, is often tolerated or overlooked. Leaders may hesitate to address such behaviors directly, fearing it could jeopardize performance or, worse, the bottom line.

His comment, "they just don't know me", stuck with me. Wasn't this the real issue? Despite comments from 18 people, he found it difficult to accept any feedback. As Carl Jung said, "*One does not become enlightened by imagining figures of light, but by making the darkness conscious.*" William's coaching journey would require him to confront uncomfortable realities about his leadership and his impact on the team. The 360-process shed light on William's empathy deficit, but we (new boss and I) needed to decide if he was ready to be coached. Before writing William off completely, I started with three questions:

1. *Ready to work with a coach to peel back the many layers of self?*
2. *Willing to do the work, committing time and effort to change?*
3. *Able to accept feedback and use it for personal growth?*

The process included narrative-based self-reflection and a career and leadership history questionnaire to increase his self-awareness. Weaving in Zaki's cognitive empathy framework and Krznaric's habits, we encouraged William to take the leap out of his comfort zone and step into the perspectives of others, (team and stakeholders). He grew frustrated with the reflective process, triggering his boss irritation. At one point, his boss pulled me aside and said, 'Can't you see this, he's dragging the team down, the finance function down and impacting not just the division but the company?'

I replied, 'To move forward is to get started. And if he'd gotten more direct feedback a long time ago, we'd be having an entirely different conversation.' The organization reinforced his behaviour for years, now unravelling that dynamic required patience and a more nuanced coaching process to help William see what others saw.

It wasn't just about William; these inclusion behaviors need to be embedded within the organization's systems and processes. That story highlighted the pitfalls of a culture that prioritized results over people, ignoring the collateral damage caused along the way. After years of being rewarded for his approach, William now needs to shift his style completely.

I've encountered this situation more times than I care to count. It's not just me, E&Y 2023 survey found that the majority (86%) of employees believe empathetic leadership boosts morale while 87% of employees say empathy is essential to create an inclusive environment. At the same time, half (52%) of employees currently believe their company's efforts to be empathetic toward employees are dishonest, up from 46% in 2021, and employees increasingly report a lack of follow-through when it comes to company promises.

Despite the challenges, the coaching was a turning point for William.

Unpacking William's Leadership Style

What I discovered is that some leaders struggle to show empathy because of underlying traits or habits. In William's case, his drive for perfection often overshadowed his ability to empathize. As he put it, 'It takes too much time.' He was also stuck in the mindset of 'no one can do it as well as I can,' a belief that fueled his perfectionism.

Let's face it, as the head of finance and tax, his focus on precision and getting everything right made sense. No one wants mistakes in tax filings or the P&L. But this relentless pursuit of perfection, reinforced by corporate culture, made it difficult for him to prioritize empathy. To shift his leadership required breaking the perfectionist habit. We used the following questions to begin that process:

- **Starting Point**: *When do you find yourself most absorbed in work?* This opens the conversation on a positive note, identifying enjoyable parts of the daily work cycle.
- **Defining Perfectionism**: *When you're really engaged at work, how does it show itself?"* This question addresses perception around perfectionism and how it influences work.
- **Reflecting on Impact**: Reflecting on the budgeting process, *how did the goal of excellence either contribute or detract from the final outcome, as well as your team's well-being?* This question examined the positive and negative impacts of perfectionism.
- **Suggest a more flexible approach:** *What if you applied the 80/20 rule, accepting that a project is complete at 80%?* This question shifts towards flexibility, to adjust the ratio to 60/40.
- **Initiating Change**: *What could you do to challenge your perfectionist tendencies?* Draw on past experiences where imperfection led to unexpected positives.

We had our ups and downs, filled with moments of doubt, as he thought about quitting many times. He's not alone. I've coached people moving into senior roles who frequently encounter scrutiny of their interpersonal skills. It can be bitter pill for a perfectionist.

It took time for William to come to terms with this but at one point he had a clarifying moment that I call a Marshall Goldsmith epiphany; *'what got you here, won't get you there.'* William recognized his past successes were of limited value in his leadership role.

William's empathy deficit is not unusual. In preparing for a workshop on team leadership in a Singapore tech firm, I'd mentioned 'empathy' and was told directly that they could not and would not measure 'feelings' and to avoid raising such questions.

When anyone asks me, 'What is the real value of empathy?' I can almost always detect a misinterpretation of the word. Jamil Zaki at Stanford University found that *"…confusion arises because empathy isn't one thing at all. It encompasses multiple ways in which we connect with others"* (HBR 2024). Zaki identifies three dimensions of empathy: emotional sharing, perspective-taking, and empathic concern. These facets highlight that empathy is both a feeling and an action, far more nuanced than simply 'being nice.'

For this team, however, they firmly believed KPIs were the only way to motivate and measure success. Perspective-taking wasn't in their DNA. Some managers who hesitate to practice empathy see it as inauthentic or a distraction from hitting targets. On the contrary strong people management is not inherently at odds with achieving KPIs. In fact, E&Y research underscores that outcomes can only improve under the guidance of an empathic, inclusive leader.

Empathy is a cornerstone of inclusive leadership (or any effective leadership, for that matter), and the good news is that it's a skill we can all develop. Building empathy starts with self-awareness, beginning with the foundational question from Chapter 3: 'Who do I want to be as a leader?' This question helps us reconnect with our values. However, practicing empathy effectively requires holding those values not abandoning them altogether, but remaining open to seeing the world through others' eyes. It's about recognizing that personal values may not always align with those of others and resisting the urge to judge. This flexibility is important in cross-cultural settings, where letting go of assumptions and understanding what drives others can open up new perspectives. Ultimately, empathy is about embracing their priorities and approach to work.

Moving from Task to Empathy: William's Shift

Recognizing the importance of empathy is one thing, but breaking old habits to build new ones is another. Change requires deliberate effort, and there's always a tension between who you are and who you're striving to become. Many of us default to familiar behaviors, even when we know growth is necessary. For William, this meant asking better questions, an approach that shifted him from being task-focused to people-focused.

One way to crack this, rather than driving the conversations fixated on outcomes, William started with questions that focused on the person in front of him, such as:

1. "What about this project has been the most challenging for you, and how has it affected you personally?" (*trust and vulnerability*)
2. "If we could change one thing about how we work, what would it be and how would it help?" (*collaborative and problem solving*)
3. "What support do you need from me to feel more successful and engaged?" *(Shifts the focus to his role as a supportive leader.)*

This shift allowed William to engage more authentically and opened for meaningful conversations. He stretched his vulnerability by asking, 'When was the last time you considered quitting?' One team member responded, 'last week,' while another admitted, 'about a month ago.' Both mentioned the relentless pace and lack of recognition as reasons for considering leaving. The honesty surprised him. Raw truths that were hard to swallow. Their candidness demonstrated why such questions are so difficult to ask. But it also created a way to voice the frustrations and discuss remedies.

The Impact of Empathetic Leadership

Adjusting his style made an impact on William and the team. The ones who once felt unrecognized began to engage more and overall team morale improved. For instance, when one team member mentioned struggling with balancing caregiving responsibilities at home, William worked with the team to reprioritize tasks and deadlines. It seems small, but this was a significant gesture reinforcing his commitment to understanding and supporting his team.

Cultivating Curiosity for Lasting Change

Looking back on empathy, historically it carries roots in art, starting with the concept of "Einfühlung," or "feeling into," used to describe the emotional connection with works of art. This idea expanded over time to include interpersonal relationships, with psychologists like Theodore Lipps theorizing that "inner imitation" of others' experiences was key to developing empathy. This historical lens reminds us that empathy has always been a blend of creativity and connection, similar to business innovation and relationship building.

More recently there's research on empathy that can be cultivated through engaging with poetry. David Comer Kidd and Emanuele Castano, researchers at the New School in the US, found that reading literary fiction enhances one's Theory of Mind (ToM) the ability to notice and understand others' emotions. Similarly, researchers Giulio Gabrieli and Gianluca Esposito at Nanyang Technology University in Singapore found that reading poetry can enhance empathic traits, helping individuals see the world from another's point of view. Poetry, like art, invites us to step into another's world and experience emotions, perspectives, and nuances we might not encounter in our daily lives.

But it's not likely William (or other leaders I've worked with) would pick up a poetry book to practice empathy. Working with William I suggested using insights from Roman Krznaric, to develop "an insatiable curiosity about the particulars of those you meet." One way to do this is:

- Spending time with team members he didn't know well.
- Practicing listening and focusing fully on conversations.
- Seeking perspectives from outside his usual (financial) circles.

Whether naturally empathetic or not, leaders can benefit from remaining curious, engaging in conversations with people outside their core group, and imagining how others feel. Poetry helps us understand that different perspectives can coexist and be equally valid. Leaders who embrace creative practices, like reading poetry or exploring art, not only enrich their own emotional intelligence but also create teams that are more innovative and connected.

Broader Implications for Organizations and Society

William's story underscores a broader organizational truth: inclusion must be embedded in the framework of leadership and culture. Empathy is not just about asking, "How are you feeling?" but about understanding the reasons behind behaviors, missed deadlines, or silence. It involves listening without planning a response, recognizing others' experiences, and applying Zaki's approach to blending empathy with critical thinking.

To bridge divides in a polarized world, Krznaric's habit #6: Inspiring an Empathic Revolution, offers a compelling challenge. Inclusive leadership requires seeing empathy not just as an emotional response but as a deliberate practice one that takes effort, reflection, and a willingness to be uncomfortable. William recognized the need for change and shifted his approach not drastically, but meaningfully. He moved from being purely focused on deadlines and numbers to paying more attention to his team's needs. While the change wasn't transformational, it was a step toward a more balanced leadership style. His story is a reminder that while empathy may be the connective tissue of a functional society, building that connection within organizations takes more than intent, it requires consistent effort, accountability, and the courage to confront one's own limitations.

In the next chapter, you'll uncover the connection between empathy and humility. While empathy opens the door to understanding and valuing diverse perspectives, humility builds on this by appreciating others' strengths and creating meaningful connections.

References

Krznaric, R. (2014). Empathy: Why it matters, and how to get it. TarcherPerigee.

Zaki, J. (2024, April 8). *How to become a more empathetic listener*. Harvard Business Review. https://hbr.org/2024/04/how-to-become-a-more-empathetic-listener

CHAPTER 5

Leading with Humility

We learn who we are by working through others' eyes.
Hermina Ibarra

Humility is one piece of the inclusive leadership puzzle, interconnected with empathy and self-awareness to create a balanced approach. As mentioned earlier, self-awareness helps leaders recognize both strengths and limitations. Demonstrating humility requires empathy, which enables leaders to connect meaningfully with others. Together, these qualities provide the basis of inclusion. Across cultures and throughout history, humility has been universally recognized as a virtue, rooted in Confucian philosophy, echoed in Plato's dialogues, and valued in both spiritual traditions and leadership practices.

Just as humility has historical roots, inclusion is a basic human value that has evolved over time. More than a corporate initiative, it is a timeless leadership principle. Confucius emphasized *ren* (humaneness) and ethical leadership through harmony and mutual respect. Plato argued that governance should serve the collective good, guided by wisdom and fairness an early nod to inclusive decision-making. Aristotle similarly stressed that mutual respect is essential for leadership and community. A thread weaving these traditions together humaneness, respect, and fairness, the ingredients of inclusive leadership.

Building on this, Edgar Schein expands the concept with *here-and-now humility*, the recognition that we depend on others for knowledge, skills, and insights. This perspective shifts humility from a static trait to a relational practice, reinforcing its role in inclusive leadership. And the way we work today.

Humility Across Cultures: A Leadership Balance

In my research on humility across cultures in Asia, I found that while humility is valued across all Asian cultures, even in those with high power distance, its true impact depends on how organizational culture reinforces its application. Research by Xu (2019) highlights that the acceptance or rejection of humble leadership is often dictated by organizational norms rather than cultural values alone.

For example, in China, the perception of humble leadership depends on how employees view their leader's authority. Humility is well received when a leader is also seen as authoritative and competent, reinforcing their credibility. However, in highly collaborative environments, humility without an element of assertiveness can sometimes be misinterpreted as a lack of strength.

Similarly, in Japan, humility is embedded in corporate identity, particularly in long-established sogo shosha, where it is tied to ethical leadership, respect, and trust. Here, humility is not just a personal virtue but a business principle, emphasizing valuing others and contributing beyond oneself. Besides the Inclusive Leadership Compass assessment, the Hogan Leadership Series (2023) also examined humility from a different perspective, finding that Japanese leaders tended to score lower on the value of 'recognition'. This suggests a stronger preference for humility over self-promotion, indicating that Japanese leaders may place less emphasis on seeking external acknowledgment for their contributions.

In contrast, in the U.S., organizations often prize competition, assertiveness, and high performance, making humility in leadership more complicated. While humility can at times be misinterpreted as a sign of weakness, research by Schein, Hess, and Van Tongeren suggests that achieving the right balance of humility is critical. The challenge lies in navigating this middle ground, too little humility can be perceived as arrogance, while too much can make a leader seem ineffective or lacking influence.

Beyond leadership, Van Tongeren's work underscores how humility shapes environments where diverse perspectives are not just tolerated but valued. In an era of rapid technological, cultural, and social change, intellectual humility is no longer optional, it is indispensable. It requires leaders to acknowledge what they do not know, remain open to learning, and seek insights from others.

But humility extends far beyond professional settings. In cultural, political, and religious spheres, it enables individuals to recognize the limits of their own perspective and engage constructively with those who see the world differently. Cultural humility shifts the focus from asserting one's own worldview as correct to understanding that multiple perspectives hold value. At a time when polarization is intensifying, humility is not about retreating from difficult conversations, it is about approaching them with curiosity rather than certainty, listening rather than reacting, and seeing the humanity in others even when we disagree. This is the essence of inclusive leadership, creating space for multiple voices, learning from differences, and making decisions that reflect a broad range of perspectives.

As workplaces and societies become more interconnected, humility is not just a personal virtue but a defining characteristic of inclusive organizational cultures. Humble leaders recognize they don't have all the answers, which makes them more open to learning from others and more willing to adjust their thinking.

This tension surfaced when I coached women leaders in Korea. Several expressed concern that "openly admitting my limitations could be a career-limiting move." Finding the balance between too little and too much humility often creates friction. Is this a gender issue? Perhaps. But I've seen the same tension play out across cultures and among both men and women.

I also coached the head of sales in Thailand at a global technology company who had recently been promoted to lead a business in Singapore. Despite his strong track record in sales, his humble, low-key leadership style was seen by some as a sign of weakness—even as others viewed it as a mark of maturity. His experience underscored how perceptions of humility are shaped by context, and how, when humility is embedded in organizational culture, it becomes an asset rather than a vulnerability.

This reflects Xu's (2019) research on humility and organizational cultures: in flexible, autonomous organizations, leader humility is often viewed positively. Conversely, in mechanistic structures with rigid hierarchies, it is more likely to be seen as a weakness or diminished in value. We see this dynamic in global leadership examples, leaders like Satya Nadella at Microsoft and Mary Barra at General Motors have been praised for their humility and focus on empathy, reinforcing how these qualities are integral to their companies' cultures and long-term business success.

Edward Hess and Katherine Ludwig's book "Humility is the New Smart" argues that humility and emotional intelligence stand out as vital attributes for leadership, particularly in navigating fast-paced AI-driven technological change. Edgar Schein's "Humble Inquiry: The Gentle Art of Asking Instead of Telling" views humility as prioritizing relationships over hierarchies and advocating for adaptability, openness, and a more personalized approach. Both interpretations connect to inclusion particularly when embedded in organisational culture.

However, Schein, Hess, and Ludwig define humility as having an accurate self-assessment, a perspective I fully agree with. You might assume that self-promotion, showcasing expertise, or exercising intelligence would be the natural reaction to AI disruption. In the age of AI transformation and rapid workplace change, let's face it, leaders can no longer rely solely on their own knowledge.

Schein breaks down humility into three types: (1) basic, (2) optimal, and (3) here-and-now. He suggests that here-and-now humility is essential, the ability to balance both a command-and-control style with humility. That caught my attention, as I often have coaching clients practice and stumble through this balance.

Hess and Ludwig outline behaviors connect closely with the Inclusive Leadership Compass focus areas such as:

Hess/Ludwig	ILC
Quieting the ego	Humility
Managing self	Self-Awareness
Reflective listening	Openness
Otherness	Respect

Practicing Schein's here-and-now humility, in the moment, requires you to consciously take a pause, an almost Zen-like observation, where listening takes precedence over talking, and where you acknowledge you don't have all the answers, moving others into a more collective problem-solving mode. For some leaders, I've coached, this is really hard to do.

It certainly makes sense but is far from easy. Practicing any degree of humility means less self-focus and more 'other focus' on contributions.

If you're the expert in the meeting, shifting from having all the answers to guiding the discussion with questions, such as, 'What might we be missing?' This not only creates space to learn from others but also unlocks collective wisdom sitting with you in the room.

When you're in the bump and grind, demonstrating humility is hardly top of mind. When was the last time you were in a heated discussion over a complex problem? In that moment of high emotions, were you able to step back, let go of your status, expertise, and knowledge, and let others step in so you could listen? Anyone who can easily say 'yes' is someone I'd like to meet, as I haven't come across him or her yet.

Given the complexities and uncertainties of business today, mastering the here and now humility is something everyone needs to learn, the balance of sharing expertise and maintaining humility. To do so in a structured hierarchy, among diverse cultural groups is a delicate art. But I've seen some master it much more adeptly than others.

Schein wrote that *"This kind of humility is difficult to learn because in achievement-oriented cultures where knowledge and the display of humility is admired, being Here and Now Humble implies a loss of status."* (pg. 17). Think about it, wasn't every company you've worked for achievement focused? How can you balance the tension between humility and achievements?

I've noticed technically proficient leaders hesitate when trying to demonstrate humility, being vulnerable, or admitting mistakes. Is this hesitation rooted in cultural norms, the nature of work, or incentive programs that prioritize excellence above all? My hunch is that it's the organizational culture and reward systems that not only shapes but reinforces this tendency.

Here's one example of how this tension plays out at work.

I worked with Simon, head of Compensation and Rewards at a global luxury brand in Shanghai, and this engagement had the challenges working across cultures, navigating technical excellence, and humility. Simon was originally from the UK, spent his formative years in Hong Kong, fluent in Cantonese and Mandarin, gifted in math, graduate of the Wharton School. He'd previously worked with multinationals in the US, Europe and Africa. Before taking on his current role. He was quite good cross-culturally, but under stress his cultural aptitude diminished. What stood out about Simon was his knack for numbers and data.

In stakeholder interviews, Simon's boss described him as 'sui generis', 99.9% right when it came to C&R issues. Others described him as affable and prickly at the same time. Colleagues described Simon as personable yet occasionally irritable. Outside of work he was the funny guy and always kind to a fault. Professionally it was all work, focused and standoffish. He was complex, both approachable and remote, a blend of "Jekyll and Hyde" persona depending on the situation.

In small groups, he presented well and could make the complex easy, a great leadership quality. That was his gift. Simon worked in a world of actuarial and compensatory spreadsheets and numbers, which he thoroughly enjoyed. During a recruitment drive for one of the business units, the China MD asked for his help to revamp their sales compensation. They were about to roll out a new brand and the MD was concerned about their inability to attract talent, compounded by a high turnover on the sales team.

Simon worked with the China MD to design a competitive compensation strategy and over many months partnered with external consultants to collect the data. For Simon, this wasn't just another assignment, it was exactly the kind of challenge he was built for. The global head of HR knew this compensation strategy would have enterprise-wide implications across business functions and brands. There was likely to be resistance. He told Simon test the idea with a few internal stakeholders to get preliminary feedback and buy-in. Simon agreed but never acted on this advice, saying to a colleague, 'feedback is for those who aren't sure of their work. I don't need to test it out, it would be more a formality than a necessity.'

Simon was intense, data driven and fully believed in the accuracy of well-formulated data. He didn't see the need to even get anyone's buy-in, that his analytic ability would easily impress or overwhelm and secure the necessary approval. He rarely shared his research and was territorial about his work. He knew the data and was confident when presenting his numbers.

(Yes, there are people that do work that way.)

The China MD told him to connect with some of the functional leaders to get input. 'Thanks, but that could delay the project. I'm 100% certain this is the right strategy; I've done the math, and the math doesn't lie.' When an opportunity to meet some of the other functional teams.

Simon excused himself, saying to his boss, 'small talk is just not my thing; I need to focus on this project.'

Six months into the Simon's research, the MD asked him to present it to the executive team during an offsite in Hangzhou. He was ready to do so, having meticulously organized all the data points. All the numbers added up.

He confidently walked into the meeting room, opened his laptop and showed the first slide, which was a mosaic of numbers and data points. He launched into his presentation and never stopped. For Simon, every chart, every graph, every statistic were ones he knew intimately and almost came to life when he showed them.

Everyone started to lose interest except for the Finance VP. A few tried to ask questions, but Simon told them to wait until he finished. At the end of the presentation, the Finance VP challenged him on some of the data, saying there may well have been a formulaic error on slide number 33. That opened the floodgates, others chiming in with questions and critiques. The questions triggered Simon's reaction, which could have been either fight, flight, or figure-it-out. You can likely guess which one. Instead of a 'figure it out' in real time, Simon went into flight mode. He took a deep breath, glanced over at the China MD for support but the MD had been scrolling through his messages and politely excused himself to head into another meeting. Simon shut down physically and mentally. He closed his laptop, said nothing, and abruptly left the room shortly after the MD.

When he returned to Shanghai, the HR head asked how it went. "It was brutal. I wasn't ready to have been bombarded with questions and they were hostile. And to make it worse, the MD left in the middle of the Q&A session. No support. I felt like a trapped animal."

The compensation project was put on hold. Recruitment stalled, turnover increased, the brand rollout was delayed and unsurprisingly Simon was disengaged and felt undervalued.

It was then when Simon's boss asked me to work with him. They didn't want to lose him, but weren't sure if coaching would help. I believe *everyone* has the potential to grow and develop but also knew this would take time. This coaching engagement required an open collaboration of Simon's boss, Simon, and me.

When we first met, Simon said, "I know what I'm doing. I don't need support. Not from you or anyone else."

"Alright then, how would you like to move forward.... Or not?"

"As I said, I'm fine. I know exactly what I'm doing. It will take time, but they'll come around. They don't understand data. And even if they did, I honestly don't go around showing the charts to everyone."

"Can I test your assumptions on that comment, 'they don't understand?'"

"Look, if the MD hadn't left that meeting in Hangzhou none of this would have happened and I wouldn't even be talking to you. OK?"

That's how we began.

Under stress, the other side of Simon's personality surfaced. He was building the best database and piece of research known to mankind but left mankind out of the process. After his presentation, he was labeled as stubborn and arrogant. He didn't agree, convinced he was right and that everyone else was too slow to understand.

Simon did, however, have a humble side; he just needed to reconnect with it. At the beginning of the coaching engagement, he pulled out the results of an earlier Hogan Leadership Assessment that offered insights into his developmental opportunities. He hadn't acted on these, instead stored them away in a folder on his laptop labeled, 'to read later' His Hogan showed that under stress his confidence went into overdrive, so he was easily seen as haughty and resistant to feedback.

Perceptions matter, and make a significant difference, particularly with inclusive leaders. In Marshall Goldsmith's book, *Mojo, How to Get It, How to Keep It, How to Ge it Back If You Lose It,* he has a perspective on perceptions and reputations. "*It's where you add up who you are (identity) and what you've done (achievements) and toss the combined sum out into the world to see how people respond.*"

I'd add two layers to Goldsmith's description.

First is to see how others respond when you're under pressure, when your strengths, such as confidence, are overused and interpreted as arrogant. This was exacerbated by Simon's independence and preference to work alone.

The second is cultural: it's about how perceptions and overused strengths are interpreted differently across contexts. In Simon's case, his confidence, which he viewed as a strength, was perceived by others as arrogance. His presentations often showcased his expertise with numbers and data, but he didn't leave time for questions. While his confidence might have been appreciated in some settings, in this culture, it came across as dismissive and inflexible. Whether or not Simon agreed with these perceptions, they lingered and shaped how others engaged with him, often more than the reality of his intentions.

I've observed how perceptions impact careers, and in Simon's case, his humility was overshadowed by what others saw as arrogant confidence an image of self-importance that became more pronounced under pressure. His strengths, when overplayed, worked against him. This perception was further exacerbated by his solitary work style and reluctance to build a network, leaving him struggling to build alliances for his project or gain support from anyone besides the China MD.

Resistance to Networks: A Case in Practice

To reconnect with his humble side, drawing inspiration from Edgar Schein, Simon had to build connections and engage others before his next presentation, regardless of their knowledge in C&R. It started with having a meeting before the meeting. This "pre-meeting preparation" was shared early in my career on a 12 hour flight to Los Angeles by a seasoned executive with a global entertainment firm. "Meetings," he explained, "are for details, numbers, and confirmation. The real work helping people connect to your project and how you plan to deliver it happens long before that." He viewed these pre-meetings as 'sacred' behind-the-scenes conversations as laying the groundwork and giving people time to think. When the formal meeting takes place, just about everyone is bought in and can add to the conversation. He emphasized, 'this isn't about status or authority but about creating space for substantial dialogue. "You have to find the time early on for productive disagreement," he said. "This makes the ideas more durable.

The idea of building a network to test his idea was completely outside Simon's comfort zone, he preferred relying on data. So in turn, I used data to move him from being a solo operator to building a network (what researchers call "building social capital"). Drawing on the research of Inga Carboni, Rob Cross, and Ron Burt, I recommended a more structured and research-driven approach to developing these skills. This included identifying informal influencers across a diverse group of stakeholders and creating broader connections across the firm.

Since Simon began with limited connections, we focused on identifying and bridging structural holes, a term coined by Ron Burt (1992) to describe gaps in a social network where connections are missing. Using Burt's concept, Simon was able to get his head around reaching beyond a close-knit group of like-minded compensation experts to build a diverse network of individuals he wouldn't normally connect with or engage in conversation.

It took some time for Simon to see the value of connecting with people who were not directly linked, to access new information and viewpoints to make it more effective in selling his idea. If he had this network in place, he would have walked into the previous meeting with broader support, which is always an advantage when lobbying for a change, particularly a compensation strategy.

The breadth and diversity of your network is critical for navigating organizational dynamics and perceptions. It requires going beyond your immediate circle to build meaningful connections. In Simon's coaching engagement, we focused on two areas for building and measuring humility: (1) Networks and (2) Perception Management.

As Schein pointed out, this type of humility would have required Simon to rely on others to align on the project. His boss had advised the same, but Simon was uncomfortable with the idea. To him, it felt like lobbying for something that was already logical and backed by data. The thought of lobbying, or having a "meeting before the meeting," felt like a colossal waste of time. Looking back, though, even a few informal conversations could have strengthened support for his strategy and softened any negative perceptions about him.

So, how is this actually done? Ron Burt's research on network analysis provided Simon with a practical, research-based starting point. The idea was simple: map out all his potential connections, influencers, and decision-makers for his project. Then, identify structural holes by asking, Who's missing?

Here's the process we worked through together:

1. **Evaluate Network Structure**: We assessed Simon's network to identify gaps in expertise, function, and level. Was his network diverse or concentrated within one Business Unit? Asking these questions revealed gaps and helped pinpoint areas needing attention.
2. **Leverage and Connect**: We found ways for Simon to bridge network gaps by connecting with key stakeholders, like the China MD or Finance VP. This wasn't about introductions but aligning shared priorities and demonstrating his value.
3. **Strategize and Diversify**: We identified overlapping connections and sought perspectives or resources Simon lacked. This step tested Simon's humility, requiring him to acknowledge gaps in his network and consider the possibility of learning from others. The goal was

to build a network that would actively support and advocate for his project.
4. **Plan for a Strategic Network**: Finally, we helped Simon step out of his comfort zone to intentionally expand relationships. This meant taking a systemic approach, connecting across all levels and functions to understand the impact of his compensation project on the broader organization.

Here's the thing: no project inside an organization exists in isolation. Simon knew this but hadn't taken steps to include others. His compensation project had implications that spanned levels, functions, and other business units. One goal of this network exercise was to help Simon see the interconnections across the firm and recognize the opportunity to learn from others. Knowing the importance of networks is one thing, but knowledge alone doesn't help—you need to build your network early, so it's there when you need it. This is where inclusion and humility come into play. You might be the expert, but you need to stay open to other perspectives. Doing so not only improves the project's outcomes but also builds alliances and support for your ideas.

Since Simon would likely face similar challenges in future projects, our coaching focused on overcoming this stumbling block, starting small. Could he have conversations with others outside his scope of expertise? Would he listen and value the contributions others could bring to his project?

Simon began making regular, brief calls with team members and made himself available for other projects where his expertise could be valuable, gradually extending his comfort zone. He consciously worked to consider the viewpoints of others, especially those without his technical knowhow. As mentioned earlier, Simon could be quite funny outside of work. During the China MD's offsite, he facilitated workshops, shared his expertise, and connected with colleagues on a more personal level, all while balancing his preference for autonomy.

The theory of structural holes made sense to Simon. He managed to get his project back on track. His now diverse network, rather than a tightly knot one, opened up more opportunities and innovative ideas for this project. We also used this network to unpack perceptions with three key questions:

1. **What do I want others to remember about working with me?** The comments after his first presentation, along with self-reflection, helped Simon answer this question.
2. **Where might there be gaps between how I see myself and how others see me?** Simon used a smaller group of trusted advisors in his network to address perceptions, asking what am I known for?
3. **How can I make my intentions clearer through my interactions?** Deliberate actions from Simon's informal network reinforced his goal to be seen as an expert advisor and inclusive leader.

Using these questions stretched Simon's humility, as it required him to confront how others perceived him and consider actions he might otherwise dismiss as spin doctoring or inauthentic. This discomfort is common in leaders, particularly those who prefer to rely on their expertise alone. Perception management is a critical aspect of leadership, especially inclusive leadership, as it speaks to intention versus impact and how others see and support your vision.

In my doctoral research, I examined the importance of information networks for women in leadership. Just about everyone I interviewed said, without this network, I wouldn't be where I am today. I also recognized the value at work, facilitating talent management discussions for a global entertainment firm in the Asia Pacific Region. When someone's name was brought up for a role, I'd often hear leaders say, *"I'm not certain I know Mr. or Ms. X. I've checked my network, and they don't know this person either."* Alternatively, they might make a comment about perceptions: *"I don't think Mr. or Ms. X is good at this because…"* These observations spotlighted a recurring issue: the invisibility of individuals within these informal, influential networks and how perceptions, accurate or not, can impact opportunities or derail a career.

For underrepresented or geographically dispersed groups, this invisibility is particularly damaging. Even if individuals possess the right skills or qualifications, being outside these core networks often leaves them subject to assumptions. This further underscores the importance of perception management, as it aligns how others experience your intentions and abilities with your desired outcomes. Leaders need to actively shape and manage perceptions, not only to increase their visibility but also to build credibility. Without connections to core networks or recognition from decision-makers, leaders' risk being overlooked especially in talent management discussions. From an inclusive talent perspective, leaders and others in the discussion need to consider who's missing from the talent plans and promotion discussions.

As Daniel Goleman highlights in his first book on emotional intelligence, these invisible, informal networks function like the nervous system of an organization, connecting people in ways that formal structures cannot. They enable the flow of information and collaboration that is critical not only to the success of projects but also to careers, organizational efficiencies, and enhancing inclusion. As seen with Simon, these networks go beyond formal boundaries and create opportunities to sell ideas and improve them.

In my dissertation, I read Ronald Burt's research, which demonstrates how networks of relationships and connections facilitate access to resources, enhancing a leader's efficiency and effectiveness. Through correspondence with Burt, I discovered the unique ways informal networks affect women in leadership, and how it differs from male leadership experience and across different cultures. Burt's (1998) research, *The Gender of Social Capital*, explores how social networks create competitive advantages and how these dynamics differ by gender. Additionally, Fanny M. Cheung and Diane F. Halpern's (2008) book, *Women at the Top: Powerful Leaders Tell Us How to Combine Work and Family*, provides insights into the challenges and strategies of top-level women leaders. Cheung, a professor at the Chinese University of Hong Kong, has extensively researched gender studies and women's leadership, offering valuable perspectives on the importance of networks in women's career advancement. I've observed that a lack of access to these networks often limits the progress of women and other marginalized groups. By analyzing networks, we can identify and address inclusion gaps.

Since then, I've realized one of the biggest opportunities for inclusion lies in examining how individuals interact and communicate within an organization. People don't interact (and might not have the opportunity to interact) with everyone equally, which leads to the formation of closed clusters and restricts visibility. Informal, interconnected networks are essential to every organization's structure, as they represent the diverse and necessary layers of interaction. While it's easy to map formal networks, these are only a fragment of a much more complex ecosystem.

One methodology addressing these inclusion gaps is Organizational Network Analysis (ONA). It uses technology tools to provide a visual representation of connections and information flows across an organization. For leaders like Simon, who often operate in silos or rely heavily on expertise alone, tools like ONA highlight the importance of connection and visibility in achieving leadership impact. The great part about ONA is its ability to identify where influencers and decision-makers are located, shedding light on the networks that Simon had to navigate and engage with to improve his reputation and credibility. Organizations like GM, Microsoft, and Cisco Systems use ONA for various purposes, but more importantly, to strengthen inclusion and talent management. ONA can improve onboarding by assessing the breadth of connections new employees establish, which is critical to their success in the first year. It also helps identify barriers to inclusion by mapping areas of exclusion, revealing opportunities to create a more inclusive and connected workplace.

In their article, *Mapping Exclusion* (2021), Inga Carboni, Andrew Parker, and Nan Langowitz demonstrated how ONA pinpoints opportunities to strengthen inclusivity. It clarifies the effectiveness of sponsorship in developing connections and enhancing diversity while identifying individuals who can drive inclusion efforts. Just as Simon began to strategically leverage his network to shift perceptions and build credibility, ONA reveals how mapping talent across networks and uncovering interconnections can drive more inclusive talent management practices. ONA demonstrates the importance of professional connections in career progression but the value of data-driven approaches to improving inclusion.

But it requires action. Using ONA data effectively is essential for making a measurable impact. When I consulted with a tech firm in Singapore, their HR team used ONA to identify patterns of disconnect among women and other underrepresented groups, particularly those separated geographically or working in different functions and levels. The findings revealed clear gaps and actionable insights, much like the gaps in Simon's informal network. The real challenge was moving beyond analysis to action. We later found that no one acted on the data. All the tools and insights in the world won't drive change unless someone takes responsibility to act on them.

This is a common pitfall, whether using ONA, perception management, unconscious bias training, or even coaching. Awareness alone isn't enough; action bridges the gap between insight and real change. For Simon, acting on his network gaps meant building credibility within his informal network and demonstrating his expertise and intentions consistently. For the tech firm, acting on the ONA data would have meant:

- Improving metrics for tracking talent progress and refining the definition of leadership to better identify potential leaders.
- Designing network strategies and making targeted introductions to integrate underrepresented groups into core (decision-making) networks.

These interventions not only address immediate challenges but also create systemic change opening pathways and reshaping organizational practices to be more inclusive. Leaders, like Simon, must confront the discomfort of stepping outside their areas of expertise to engage in the broader community that influences visibility and credibility.

Humility is the glue that binds self-awareness and empathy to create meaningful connections. As Simon's coaching journey illustrated, strengthening humility and valuing external perspectives were critical in shifting perceptions and driving inclusion. His experience reflects what Edgar Schein describes as here-and-now humility, the recognition that leadership is not about having all the answers but about being open to learning from others in the moment. It took repeated nudges, reflection, and deliberate action for Simon to expand his relationships across the firm. He not only changed how he was perceived but also unlocked more of his own potential. His journey underscores a simple truth, as Herminia Ibarra states: *"We learn who we are by working through others' eyes."* And Simon achieved more than just learning by actively building relationships with others.

In the next chapter, we look at onboarding practices and their vital connection to networks. Onboarding isn't just about acclimating new employees, it's about helping them establish the connections they need to succeed on day one. We also consider cross-cultural elements in talent management and leadership approaches. Using the Inclusive Leadership Compass and Kline's Thinking Environment as frameworks, we unpack the nuances of communication and leadership styles and examine how these differences influence career advancement.

REFERENCES

Burt, R. S. (1998). The gender of social capital. Rationality and Society, 10(1), 5–46. https://doi.org/10.1177/104346398010001001

Burt, R. S. (1992). *Structural Holes: The Social Structure of Competition*. Harvard University Press.

Carboni, I., Parker, A., & Langowitz, N. S. (2021). Mapping exclusion in the organization. MIT Sloan Management Review. https://sloanreview.mit.edu/article/mapping-exclusion-in-the-organization/

Cheung, F. M., & Halpern, D. F. (2008). *Women at the top: Powerful leaders tell us how to combine work and family*. Oxford University Press.

Xu, S. (2019) A Review of the Effectiveness and Boundary Conditions of Leader Humility. Journal of Service Science and Management, 12, 234–245. https://doi.org/10.4236/jssm.2019.122016

PART III

Inclusive Systems and Career Pathways

CHAPTER 6

Addressing Inclusion Gaps in Organisational Systems

Attention is the rarest and purest form of generosity
Simone Weil

In the previous chapters, we examined the self, other, and team dimensions of inclusion by examining generative listening, creating connections, and building trust. Now, we shift our attention to the organizational focus area of the Inclusive Leadership Compass, with a specific emphasis on onboarding and talent management. This is where I've seen inclusion falling through the cracks and research supports this observation.

Why this matters? Gallup found that 34% of employees report never receiving any onboarding program, and only 29% feel prepared for their roles after onboarding. In talent management, the data reveals another disturbing trend: women are more likely to opt out of the leadership pipeline at pivotal stages, according to Visier.

Additionally, Deloitte's Asia Pacific Impact Report highlights efforts for Women in Technology with tailored development opportunities for mid-career women however data on other underrepresented groups remains limited. Deloitte's findings suggest that even with programs targeting diverse talent at entry-level positions, many women still leave tech roles before reaching leadership ranks. This underscores the ongoing challenges in retaining diverse talent and embedding inclusion throughout the employee lifecycle. Similarly, **DDI** research highlights that women hold just 24% of senior leadership roles, often due to systemic

© The Author(s), under exclusive license to Springer Nature
Singapore Pte Ltd. 2026
J. Horan, *Coaching Inclusion*,
https://doi.org/10.1007/978-981-95-0265-3_6

barriers in identifying and promoting talent. Over the past decade, McKinsey, Lean In and DDI have consistently assessed barriers women have faced when advancing through the corporation.

These findings reflect a broader issue I've consistently observed, not only for women but also for other underrepresented groups. While hiring diverse talent is important, the real opportunity lies in creating an environment where that talent can grow, develop, and advance. Through my work with organizations and research on women in leadership, I've noticed a similar pattern an overemphasis on recruiting diverse talent without the same effort to reevaluate systems and processes to retain that talent and support their success.

This includes designing an onboarding plan, developing inclusive leaders, listening for what's different, and recognizing unique strength. Without an inclusive strategy that reexamines talent, performance, and leadership selection criteria, companies risk losing not only the benefits of diversity but also their investment in talent.

When talented individuals are overlooked or leave, the cost goes beyond low engagement scores, it affects the firm's business outcomes. This chapter examines two often overlooked areas: the role of informal networks and the need to refresh leadership criteria.

As highlighted in the previous chapter, networks are essential for selling ideas, managing perceptions, and driving inclusion within the talent process. Yet they are frequently undervalued as critical drivers of inclusion. Similarly, outdated leadership frameworks can impede the identification and development of future talent. By rethinking these frameworks and leveraging networks, inclusion becomes embedded in the organization's DNA.

Inclusion Begins with Understanding

You've heard this before; inclusion starts with taking a hard look at yourself in order to understand others. A simple phrase, but when we scale it to where policy and practice intertwine, it becomes far more demanding. Onboarding is the earliest opportunity to integrate inclusion, and many organizations proudly tout their onboarding programs, but it's often where they falter.

When IKEA experienced high turnover among new hires, they introduced a peer support program, pairing new employees with more experienced colleagues who acted as a go-to resource for questions, concerns and to understand the corporate dynamics. This served as a bridge offering guidance, building relationships, and ultimately reducing early turnover while laying the groundwork for long-term engagement and stability (Woosley 2024).

In contrast, I worked with a global FMCG company headquartered in Switzerland where onboarding failures created disengagement and early turnover. A higher number than usual of new employees were leaving after 3–6 months. HR and hiring managers attributed it to entry-level salaries, as they'd been told their compensation wasn't competitive. However, exit interviews revealed a different story. Employees weren't leaving for better pay, as some even accepted roles with lower salaries. They were leaving because they felt disconnected and excluded. Everything pointed to the firm's culture and culture starts with leadership. In the following sections, I'll share how we looked at the root cause and shifted the process.

CULTURE STARTS WITH LEADERSHIP

Two newly hired employees on their consumer insights team shared their experiences with me. During the interviews they found one of the senior leaders from the Switzerland headquarters was personable and engaging, they were excited to join. After starting they rarely heard from him and assumed it was due to geographic distances. In Zoom meetings he presented leaving little time for questions or engaging with anyone new on the team. HR mentioned he would be in Singapore for a meeting the following week. While most of the office worked remotely, everyone returned to the office when he arrived.

"We were excited to finally meet him in person. We got to the office early." One of the new hires recalled that, 'He walked past us in the hallway without a word, as though we didn't exist. Then he went straight into the conference room and announced a major decision about the firm relocating to Switzerland without any discussion or explanation. The other added, "We weren't just ignored. We were invisible."

This wasn't just any leader; it was the warm and engaging senior hiring manager. His sudden shift in behavior wasn't just a failure of inclusion, it was a complete disconnect from the expectations of leadership. This behavior raised more questions about how this leaders' actions reflect (or fail to reflect) the culture an organization claimed to embody.

That evening, the team, without the boss, went out for drinks to either commiserate or celebrate. For the new hires, the drinks became a way to bond. While they found the leader's behavior odd, the more tenured staff had a different perspective. "It used to be worse", one said. Another long-standing team member chimed in, "Oh yeah, we learned early on that if you haven't been here for at least a year or don't have experience in the beverage industry, your opinions don't matter." Then another added, "It takes time, but leadership is improving. He used to visit Asia far less frequently, and the fact that he's showing up more often now, even on Zoom, is progress, albeit slow."

Little consolation. His indifference made the situation worse. His preference for familiar faces sent a clear message about who was valued and whose contribution mattered. The heavy investment in recruitment didn't last. A rigorous recruitment process with eight to ten interviews, global assessments and presentations meant little when a new hire's experiences were that of exclusion.

The Cost of Exclusion

Looking back on Chapter 2, *Exclusion: The Silent Disruptor* illustrates how exclusionary leadership behaviors, whether intentional or unintentional, can harm a company's reputation and bottom line. When leaders are unwilling to trust people outside their industry or value their contributions, the organization suffers.

The tenured employees' comments about how "it takes time" to be heard point to systemic issues in the firm. A culture that prioritizes tenure and familiarity stifles innovation and ultimately limits business outcomes and competitive advantage.

This resistance is akin to an ecosystem rejecting something new, expecting employees to adapt and fit into existing norms rather than integrating fresh perspectives. Instead of being inclusive and accepting of difference, such cultures push individuals to change in order to be accepted. As seen in the first story in this chapter, a leader's inability to listen to new employees not only excluded their ideas ultimately undermined the organization's investment in this talent. The firm spent considerable time and money recruiting new talent but failed to benefit from this investment by prioritizing tenured voices. Surprisingly enough this is common. Facilitating an inclusive leadership workshop with a global NGO, a couple of participants introduced themselves as being new; one joined 3 years prior, the other joined 18 months earlier. Both said, 'we're new, still learning how things work here but we know not to say anything." Three years in, and still 'new'? That's a lost opportunity, not onboarding.

Working for a global consumer products firm illustrates the cost of exclusion. The organization noticed an unusually high turnover within the first 3–6 months of employment. There was a significant uptick on new employees leaving shortly after completing their initial training. Looking into the details, the company discovered it was spending over $20 million on training programs during the first few months of employment. These programs focused almost exclusively on technical skills and job-specific knowledge, with little attention paid to helping employees learning how to navigate the firm. As a result, the $20 million investment yielded little ROI, as employees left before they could fully contribute to the organization. This misalignment between onboarding practices and retention goals demonstrated how costly a lack of inclusion and effective onboarding can be, not financial but also in loss in unrealized potential.

Building Inclusive Cultures: Reshaping Onboarding and Leadership Practices

As I reflected on this experience (and others), the value of onboarding became even clearer. A wholistic process not only helps new employees navigate the organization but also enables them to feel part of the organization early on. That said, it's not just about onboarding, it's about leadership. For the FMCG firm, the lack of inclusion wasn't only a gap in their processes, it was a direct reflection of leadership behaviors. Leaders play a significant role in building an inclusive culture. It's not a single step but a consistent practice woven throughout the employee lifecycle.

Networks: The Silent Engine for Inclusion

Many organizations underestimate the power of informal networks particularly in on-boarding and talent management. Yet these networks act as arteries, connecting different functions, helping employees sell ideas and, more importantly, supporting new hires in successfully transitioning into their roles. Research shows that the quality of a new hire's network is far more important than the number of people they meet in the first few months. Despite all of these insights and data informal networks are often overlooked in onboarding.

A simple redesign of the onboarding process addresses this gap by creating an integrated, holistic approach. This includes:

- Facilitating cross-functional introductions.
- Providing structured time to meet with key stakeholders and decision-makers.
- Offering guidance on how to map these informal interconnections.
- Creating a visual map of relationships and information flow, either using Organizational Network Analysis (ONA) or a manually drawn network map.
- Maintaining regular touch points during the onboarding process.
- Understanding the internal and external marketplace.

The Role of Organizational Network Analysis (ONA)

Organizational Network Analysis (ONA) has proven to be an effective tool for strengthening retention for new hires and supporting employees navigating transitions. A great tool and the real value lie in translating insights into actions. One case in point, Cognitive Talent Solutions, a provider of ONA, partnered with a European IT company to predict and address attrition issues. They found that employees less connected to organizational networks were more likely to leave. Through targeted interventions, the company reduced attrition rates, improving both retention and team performance.

Rob Cross, an expert in social networks and organizational network analysis (ONA) at Babson College, has long advocated for integrating social capital into HR, DEI, and talent strategies to address these challenges. Not only do I agree with Cross, but I've applied his principles in the design of onboarding process for a global entertainment firm. The process included network mapping coupled with stakeholder questions for new employees to successfully transition into organization. Similarly, I've used this approach to coach executives during their first 100 days in leadership, helping them to build a network of advisors both internally and externally for a successful start in their new role.

It's not just onboarding; networks play an important role in talent management. Research by Carboni et al. (2021) found that using ONA can identify where high-potential candidates are missing from critical decision-making networks or highlight connections that amplify their visibility and influence. Lacking these connections, or being excluded from them, can negatively impact career progression. They observed:

> *Networks are how people learn the unwritten rules of success, hear about job and promotion opportunities before they are posted, and, most critically, build a level of interpersonal trust and rapport with their contacts that translates into a willingness to pick up the phone and vouch for someone's capabilities. According to their findings, nearly 40% of the gender pay gap can be attributed to the informal relationships men have with their male managers.* (Carboni et al. 2021)

Networks alone aren't enough to advance talent. To make the most of them, organizations need to rethink how they identify talent and redefine leadership frameworks to reflect the realities of a global workforce including the 3.5 billion people in Asia. In my experience, this is where organizations often resist change. I've worked with companies to evolve their competency frameworks, and I know from my experience that it takes time. But without this shift, organizations risk creating barriers to inclusion and losing valuable talent.

The Opportunity for Inclusive Talent Management: Rethinking Leadership

Inclusion in talent management is to recognize different leadership styles and reduce the reliance on 'presence' or 'visibility.' In working with multinationals, I've found that many use leadership models and competency frameworks rooted in Western norms, which emphasize "speaking up" and outward confidence. We need to recognize that *speaking up, presence,* and *visibility* are influenced by culture.

In my coaching practice, 'presence' is a problematic topic, highly subjective and shaped by cultural contexts. Presence in New York differs appreciably from presence in Belgium, Beijing, or Bombay, often overshadowing equally valid leadership capabilities. When I ask leaders to define presence, I rarely hear anything tangible. Indeed, if hear it in the context of a meeting with clients, a red flag goes up: a career should not hinge on vague criteria like "I'll know it when I see it," a comment I've heard all too often.

Thirty-five years ago, James M. Kouzes and Barry Z. Posner, in *The Leadership Challenge*, (1987) found that individuals who actively participated and spoke up in group settings were more likely to be perceived as leaders. From my research, I saw that women frequently faced professional setbacks and stymied advancement due to cultural and gendered biases. These perceptions of leadership are further exacerbated by an overemphasis on visibility rather than substance. While such characteristics may align with *some* leadership styles, they can also create barriers for those whose approaches differ, particularly those from cultures where leadership is expressed more collaboratively or subtly.

Inclusive Leadership isn't about fitting into an existing mold; it's about reshaping that mold to reflect the diverse realities of the workforce. A reluctance to redefine leadership leads to misjudgment about potential leaders and, in some cases, career derailment. We'll see this issue through a coaching story of Aileen, a senior leader in Hong Kong. Her leadership potential was questioned due to her quiet demeanor in Zoom meetings, which aligns with my research and Kouzes and Posner's findings.

This misjudgment stems from an overemphasis placed on traits like confidence and presence, which are often culturally biased and not necessarily predictive of leadership effectiveness. As Sally Helgesen highlights in her book *Rising Together* (2023), research shows that "competence is statistically far more aligned with and predictive of job performance than confidence or self-belief," and "multiple studies make clear that competency is actually the chief factor in determining a leader's success." In my stakeholder interviews with Aileen, this became apparent. While her quiet demeanor was misinterpreted as a lack of confidence, her competence, team engagement and ability to deliver results were consistently noted as her greatest strengths.

Like "presence," confidence is laden with cultural nuances, and relying on such subjective traits as indicators of leadership potential can marginalize highly capable individuals who do not fit conventional stereotypes. Aileen's case underscores the importance of evaluating leaders based on measurable behaviours and impact rather than subjective traits. By doing so, organizations create more inclusive definitions of leadership that reflect the workforce.

As the coaching engagement progressed, it became evident that this was less about her leadership abilities and more about the need to adopt a better understanding of what leadership looks like. Let's uncover how to overcome mis-categorization.

Removing Categories: Aileen's Story

Aileen was an optimistic, intelligent, amiable leader with a can-do attitude, the first Asian female leader in Hong Kong hired externally to join a global financial technology firm. Her boss was based in Australia and initially described Aileen to me as a humble servant leader (a description many would like to have).

"I hired Aileen and believed she has a lot more to offer" he told me. "She's has actually turned around our business in two years, hired and developed a strong team and has solved some of the messy problems she was given when she started. Her team might need some fine tuning but otherwise I give her high marks."

He continued. 'I've been working here forever and sometimes it's hard to fit in at our firm. We typically don't hire anyone from the outside, particularly senior leadership roles because, frankly, it's seldom worked. I want Aileen to succeed."

The more I listened to him, the more confused I was about what I was supposed to be coaching her on.

"She's been here over 18 months, transitioned well, delivered exceptional results, built a great team, a problem-solver" and I finally had to interject with "what more would you like to say about Aileen or this engagement?" but continued highlighting Aileen's accomplishments, nothing about the coaching focus.

I thought they were going to offer her a bigger leadership role or broaden the scope of her current role and I'd be coaching her on the next step of her career, a normal step.

I was wrong on both counts.

He then said:

"My boss, who is in Canada, isn't convinced of Aileen's leadership ability." 'Aha' I thought, 'now we're getting somewhere.'

He's more used to working with tenured employees, those he knows and likes. He's a lifer. He's got a great track record of nurturing talent and doling out opportunities to a lot of the staff. But with Aileen, I don't quite know. He questions almost everything she does. He says she's not good with presentations, and that she's too quiet on conference calls—which is not my experience. I know she's on every call, day or night, and many times he's on those calls too, more than me. But apparently, she never says a word unless asked.

(I wanted to interrupt and say: then why not ask? If speaking up is valued, why not create the space or at least extend the invitation to speak?)

He went on to say, "And when she does reply, well, it doesn't end well. So now he's almost obsessing about why she doesn't speak her mind and even telling me I may have made the wrong hiring decision, suggesting that she doesn't have what it takes to lead in our organization. That's not true. She's excellent, but I have to somehow get this resolved, for her sake and mine."

I listened, and while I then understood better about the coaching goals, thought it rash of a senior leader to dismiss her capabilities on the basis of not speaking up in a few Zoom meetings.

Aileen had that 'can-do' optimism when I first met her, and she walked into every meeting fully prepared. A Zoom meeting with 15 or more global attendees, coupled with ad hoc questions from senior leaders did not comport well with engagement and didn't demonstrate inclusion.

I wanted to shift my coaching conversation with Aileen to drill in on inclusion along with active listening to show her boss and her bosses' boss the value of asking questions without interruption (hence the active listening).

I thought leadership could take a different approach to Aileen's, or any other participant's, participation in these late-night zoom calls.

It turned out that early in the Zoom meetings, her attempts to talk were met with indifference or worse, another executive restating the same point only to be acknowledged with a flood of chat function Thumbs Up or Zoom Applause floating upwards. Aileen was perturbed and listening to everyone, was it really worth the effort to just add a comment for the sake of it? She said, *"everything's been said by others, so why bother? Besides everyone wanted to get off the call."*

Through my coaching work across multiple industries, I've seen this pattern repeatedly, and it is well-documented in research. Women's voices are often overlooked, their contributions dismissed, or their ideas credited to others. As journalist, Anjil Raval, recently wrote in the FT that "Women can find their ideas dismissed, and their contributions overlooked or attributed to others—leaving them needing to prove themselves more than male counterparts to gain the same level of respect" (Raval 2024).

In order to interrupt this pattern, I advised Aileen's boss to shift the meeting protocol to smaller groups and use more open-ended questions to get everyone involved the meeting, to speak and be heard. That would likely result in more dialogue instead of a Q&A section at the end of a Zoom call.

It made no sense to derail the career of a results-driven leader and disrupt a profitable business, all over communication style. I understood what they wanted from Aileen but thought it sensible to engage directly with the extended leadership team on behaviours of inclusion. However, that wasn't what her bosses' boss wanted from the coaching.

The coaching request was for Aileen, not for her boss or his boss. But it was hard to ignore the pattern: ".... working with tenured employees, those he "knows and likes." That's classic similarity bias, even if it wasn't named as such. And the comment that stuck with me most, *"she never says a word unless asked"* kept looping in my head.

I'm frequently asked, "How can I get my star employee to better voice their opinions?" or "How can I nudge my star performers to show some more confidence at our meetings?" Such well-meaning questions nonetheless demonstrate non-inclusive behavior reinforcing a fixed mindset about what leadership should look or talk like creating obstacles for those who don't conform to that profile. The real challenge isn't to coax someone to speak up. It is, rather, to rethink how a space can be created where employees feel genuinely invited into the conversation. Inclusion requires more than compelling someone to adapt to an existing culture; it demands an active reshaping of the lines and appreciating different leadership and communication styles.

This challenge became particularly evident coaching Aileen, whose boss had said, "I hired Aileen because I believe she has a lot more to offer." During my stakeholder interviews, everyone echoed the same comments as her boss, she's turned around the business and built a strong team."

Many organizations are reluctant-or simply cannot—adapt leadership models to accommodate diverse perspectives and styles. Aileen's experience highlights the importance of reframing the question from "How do I get my star employee to speak up?" to "How can we, as an organization include her into the conversation?" This isn't just about helping one person succeed, but about creating a workplace that's inclusive and genuinely open to different ways of contributing.

The Power of Listening: Creates an Inclusive Environment

To demonstrate my belief on the power of listening, I worked with Aileen and her boss using Nancy Kline's Thinking Environment to facilitate meetings. A few years ago, I'd read Nancy Kline's book, More Time to Think, and was struck by the connections to inclusion. Halfway through, I realized that Kline's structured listening principles and meeting protocols had the potential to transform how diverse teams communicate, collaborate, and build trust. I implemented her ideas in my coaching sessions with Aileen and soon saw significant improvements in the quality of conversations, the energy in the room, and engagement in meetings.

In David Maister's book, *The Trusted Advisor*, he writes extensively about the art of listening and its critical role in building trust. He underscored that listening goes beyond hearing words it involves understanding the emotions, motivations, and intentions behind them. *Maister writes,*

> *Why is being listened to' so important? The answer is not only about the need for rational understanding of the issues. Our desire to be heard also flows from our need for respect, empathy, and involvement. The trusted advisor recognizes this and always ensures that the self-esteem of the client is protected.* (2000, p. 98)

Maister clearly articulates what inclusion means, complementing Kline's methodology of creating environments where everyone feels heard and valued. When trust is built through meaningful listening, it lays the groundwork for inclusion, as individuals are more likely to contribute authentically and feel connected to the team. By bridging trust and inclusion, both Maister and Kline show that listening is not simply a skill but a transformative practice to grow collaboration and inclusion.

Aileen's case reinforces that the real work of inclusion goes beyond individual actions, requiring corporate cultures to value different leadership styles. Addressing systemic challenges involves deliberate steps, starting with a listening practice, where leaders demonstrate their role in driving such change. Kline's process is structured listening, paired discussions, open dialogue, behaviours that facilitate conversations where all voices are heard. Leaders should have their teams embed inclusive behaviors and address career derailments caused by numerous immeasurable factors.

These practices aren't theoretical. They're necessary.

Gallup's State of the Global Workforce (2023) report highlights the cost of disengagement: US$8.8 trillion in lost productivity, equivalent to 9% of global GDP. Adding to this, Deloitte has shown that when inclusion and trust co-exist, employee engagement rises, and talent retention improves. As early as 2015, Deloitte linked inclusive practices with trust and engagement. More recently, 2021 studies reaffirm this connection, noting that trust in DEI commitments can increase engagement by up to 20% and reduce attrition by 87%. That said, these gains may not be guaranteed in the current climate. The growing pushback on DEI in the U.S. sending shockwaves into Europe and Asia raises questions about how trust in organizational commitments can be sustained. Future research should explore how shifts in public sentiment, particularly regarding government influence, affect employee trust and perceptions of inclusion.

The first step in building trust is listening. Simple as it may seem, I've observed how Nancy Kline's Thinking Environment can change teams and MNC organizational dynamics in Asia Pacific, both virtual and in-person. It starts with asking a positive question and then sitting back to listen. More than just a pause, it's to intentionally bring the other person into the conversation and genuinely hear what they say.

By combining Kline's Thinking Environment with the trust-building principles from David Maister's The Trusted Advisor, I've gotten leaders to shape a structured and inclusive listening practice. I've highlighted it through case studies how this practice is used to equip leaders and build cultures where each voice has a value. As mentioned in Chapter 3 through Brynna's story, managers should tune into quieter team members and listen for more radical perspectives that challenge the status quo. As it should be.

At its core, inclusion is simply humanity, letting employees know you value the full spectrum of who they are. To do so requires intentional listening, resisting the urge to jump in and subtract the instinct to fill a pause with a solution. Kline (1999) calls this generative listening, being fully present, nodding without interrupting, and allowing the other person's thinking to unfold without interference. As Kline writes, *'the quality of everything we do depends on the quality of the thinking we do first. The quality of our thinking depends on the way we treat each other while we are thinking.'*

You don't need to plant questions nor plan your response.

Just listen without judging. You might be thinking, "I already do this," but I assure you that true listening is hard work and most of us don't do it as well as we think we do.

For so-called *professional listeners* like doctors, research summarized in *ScienceDaily* (2018) shows that patients are given on average, just 11 seconds to explain the reason for their visit before being interrupted. Only one in three doctors allows patients enough time to fully describe their situation. Similarly, according to the Gottman Institute (as cited in Kline 2009), the average listening time for even professional listeners was 20 seconds in 2017. Three years later, it had dropped to 11 seconds.

Across professions, counselors, teachers, leaders, and even parents, the average attention span during listening appears to be shrinking annually. While the alignment in findings may be coincidental, the insight is clear: our tendency is to listen to respond, to seek what is familiar, or to find common ground. Rarely do we listen to hear what is different.

David Maister recommended we '*listen for what's different, not what's familiar.*' Before starting a meeting or conversation, ask yourself: 'What's on the other person's mind? Where are they coming from? What challenges or emotions might they be dealing with right now?' In doing so, you're stretching your empathy muscle. Your ability to truly listen to focus on the other person's perspective without imposing your own will. To do so is to liberate both you and them.

This kind of listening doesn't come naturally because many of us were taught to offer advice, be challenging, or solve problems. But the goal is to uncover the hidden thoughts, preferences, fears, and struggles from their perspective, not ours. This listening for 'what's not familiar' is an inclusive imperative. When you listen in this manner, you genuinely model inclusion. It also shifts the dynamic, allowing the person being heard to feel valued and understood.

As Aileen and her boss practiced this method, it fundamentally changed how they interacted. Aileen's boss gained a better understanding of how she thought about the business and her leadership style, which led to a significant shift in his perception about her potential. This change didn't stop there—it also positively influenced how other stakeholders, including how her boss's boss, viewed Aileen. By creating space for Aileen's perspective to be heard, the organization began to recognize her as the capable leader she was. This was the crux of the issue: perceptions were tied not to Aileen's abilities, but to the lack of opportunity for her voice to be genuinely heard.

We've all worked with leaders who are great listeners. Have you considered what they do that makes them so? Is it a special skill? Consulting to one of the Microsoft teams in Asia, the team recanted stories read about Satya Nadella, CEO of Microsoft acute listening skills. At that time Microsoft was going through a cultural transformation and the team mentioned Nadella relied heavily on his listening skills creating an open environment where the team felt empowered to express their ideas (feelings) about this change. Nadella is egalitarian in his listening skills, known for listening across different functions and levels to understand their concerns and respond effectively. That impacts Microsoft's culture, most assuredly.

Listening to the stories on Nadella, I started to see links of Kline's listening process, which is based on a set of principles and ten behaviors, all of which enable others time to think and express themselves fully. The first is attentiveness, the second is equality, and the third is ease. One of these principles, which parallels David Maister's advice, is to "keep asking."

This doesn't mean bombarding someone with questions but rather "What would you like to think about?" and "What more are you thinking or want to say on this topic?" This second question has the ability to spark introspection and broaden perspectives.

When I first learned this practice, I struggled with asking this follow up question. To me, it felt awkward but then I saw how it changed conversations. While coaching an executive in Japan, I experienced how using Kline's process reshaped his conversations and flattened the hierarchy with his team. During one meeting, a team member had voiced dissatisfaction with the firm's delivery process. Given their hierarchical nature, it took courage. Previously, this leader might have dismissed the comment with silent disapproval or a "Let's move on."

Instead, he paused and used verbatim words from Kline's second question, asking, "What more do you think, feel or want to say about this?" After asking, he sat back and listened. Initially surprised by the leaders' question, the team member shared a detailed idea that ultimately changed how the firm delivered to a key client. A seismic cultural shift, from defending or deflecting, to listening. It created a space for innovation and broke through the hierarchical wall between leader and team.

In Kline's Thinking Environment© she has ten components which generate ideas to germinate and for people to feel their contributions matter. These components—attention, equality, ease, appreciation, encouragement, feeling, information, difference, incisive questions, and place, work together to produce a team's best thinking. For more insights on this practice, you can review the Thinking Environment site. Below are my interpretations and applications of some of these components in practice with Aileen and other clients:

- **ATTENTION**
  Kline: "listening without interruption and with interest in where the person will go next in their thinking."

  As Aileen began applying this component, she started meetings with an open question, such as "What's on your mind today?" This small but significant shift encouraged her team to share their thoughts fully and freely. Her boss recognized the impact and adopted the same approach, which then influenced how meetings were conducted at higher levels of the organization.

- **EQUALITY**
  Kline: "regarding each other as thinking peers, giving equal time to think."

  Aileen introduced the practice of giving everyone on her team an opportunity to speak and listen, regardless of rank or role. This approach helped quieter voices feel heard while encouraging more talkative individuals to pause and reflect. Aileen's boss adopted a similar approach in all cross-functional meetings, leading to better conversations and decisions across departments.

- **EASE AND ENCOURAGEMENT**
  Kline: "discarding internal urgency" and "giving courage to go to the unexplored edge of thinking by ceasing competition as thinkers."

  Aileen exemplified calm in her interactions, which in turn helped her team remain fully present in discussions. By modeling ease, Aileen inspired other cross functional leaders to be more intentional on meeting schedules. This approach was complemented her encouragement of bold thinking, which replaced a competition-drive focus with genuine support.

- **DIFFERENCE**
  Kline: "committing to freedom from untrue assumptions driving prejudice."

  Aileen's use of this component was a pivotal moment in the coaching process, as it not only shifted her team's understanding of

styles but also influenced learning across the firm. By actively challenging assumptions, she opened discussion channels that brought new perspectives and encouraged a broader appreciation for different approaches to leadership.
- **PLACE**
  Kline: "producing a physical environment, the room, the listener, your body that says, 'You matter.'"
  Aileen prioritized a welcoming environment, whether in physical spaces or virtual meetings, that communicated to her team, "You matter." Going back to the FMCG firm I mentioned, the coffee bar amid the sputtering of the expresso machine, became a central hub for meaningful conversations between executives and employees, eventually started to build a culture of connection.

In another coaching engagement I worked with John, a senior executive at an agricultural firm, and aimed to have him apply Kline's the ten components and the three-step process for meetings.

Like Aileen, John often remained quiet in meetings with senior management but dominated conversations with his team. The management team found John to be extremely hardworking, outcome-focused and highly intelligent. His team had a different view. The thought he was arrogant, always in a rush and uninterested in any office chit-chat, that it was somehow below him. He rarely gave enough time for the team to express their views, stilting their interactions.

During my stakeholder interviews, it became clear that John needed to shift how he listened and facilitated meetings. His boss identified two areas for the coaching: humility and empathy. Concepts that are easy to name but could be difficult to demonstrate. Drawing on Kline's meeting methodology and insights from Maister, I worked with John to adjust his listening style and redesign his meeting protocol to practice the coaching goals, these changes focused on three key elements.

INCLUSIVE MEETING PROCESS

1. **Clarify the Purpose**: Instead of being the sole person in charge of a meeting, John turned it to his team member to raise a topic and clarify what the outcome. Instead of John diving into a solution, he started to guide others.
   Did they want to:

(a) vent
(b) gain support
(c) provide an update
(d) co-create a solution

Following Maister's "ensuring the right to offer advice" the team member who was struggling with a supply chain problem impacting a key client, set the outcome of co-creating a solution. He wanted the team's (not John's) input to address the topic.
2. **Frame the Topic as a Question:** The next step required that the team member frame the problem as a question to facilitate discussion and generate more insights. The team member presented the purpose and objectives then asked the question: "How might we solve the supply chain issue with Client X so both the firm and the client benefit?" This question and this process of listening tilted the conversation toward creative problem-solving rather than John instructing what to do. More importantly, it demonstrated inclusion.
3. **Create a Space for Thinking**: Using this framework unlocked thinking. John practiced Kline's generative listening by nodding, avoiding interruptions, allowing time for everyone to think aloud. This simple but deliberate practice created an environment of ease, kicking around ideas without judgment or pressure. John demonstrated the ILC's focus areas: humility, openness, equality and participation.

This structured listening approach is a back-and-forth exchange that reinforces listening and makes for constructive meetings. Maister claims that consultants must earn the right to offer advice. This practice achieves that and more. I'd add that inclusive leaders must earn the right to offer advice, which is to show humility. In John's case, this meant to listen rather than tell, to listening from knowing-it—all to practicing humble inquiry.

Imagine every meeting starting with a clear topic, a defined objective, and clarifying questions. This not only improves listening but also creates a more effective, and inclusive, meeting. After all, isn't that what everyone wants? A key element of Kline's process is the use of positive questions to unlock thinking and encourage dialogue. Research highlights that the art of asking well-researched questions at the right time promotes better thinking and creativity. Positive questions, in particular, can open pathways to innovative thinking and higher engagement (Tofade et al. 2013).

Michelle Gielan, founder of the Institute for Applied Positive Research, believes meetings should begin with a "power lead", that is, a positive introduction, which is linked to increased productivity and reduced stress levels. This practice creates a space where people can stretch more freely, with positive questions guiding the process.

Using Kline's methods, the interconnecting components, creates an environment for better thinking and thus inclusion. Some components, such as Incisive Questions and Appreciation, take time to master, but I have honestly found their impact to be significant. A single, well-crafted question can move a direction, challenge and open up new possibilities.

To feel appreciated for our work is a genuine human need. If we're not delivering, then of course, we need to know. But when we do, a little recognition goes a long way. In my work with Thinking Environment Facilitators and Coaches, I've often reflected back on my time as part of an outrigger team. During paddling, I experienced the impact of receiving appreciation and acknowledgment for my efforts before any suggestions for improvement. This balance of positive feedback with constructive guidance mirrors John Gottman's 'magic ratio' of 5:1, five positive interactions for one criticism, mentioned in Chapter 3. It highlights how people are more open to receiving constructive feedback when their contributions are recognized first.

This approach works for naturally empathetic leaders. They're great at offering praise but tend to hold back when it comes to giving constructive feedback. Conversely, it's just as effective for leaders who are comfortable with constructive feedback but struggle to balance it with genuine appreciation. It's not about forcing a formulaic response but rather starting a habit of genuine acknowledgment of strengths before any constructive criticism. Over time, this approach becomes natural improving interpersonal dynamics and encouraging growth.

As a coach, you have a unique role in guiding leaders to integrate these inclusive behaviors into their leadership practices. The following actionable steps are not just organizational recommendations but coaching strategies you can use to help leaders and teams build a pipeline of inclusive talent. By working through these steps with your clients, you can help them to reframe leadership and develop systemic approaches to inclusion.

Developing an Inclusive Talent Management Process: Actionable Steps

1. Build a Global Leadership Model

    - **Coaching Opportunity:** Work with leaders to challenge culturally laden notions of leadership in their organization. Use coaching sessions to reframe leadership around competence, results, empathy, and team empowerment.
    - **Reflection Prompt:** Ask clients, "What leadership behaviours do we value in this organization? Are these measurable?"

2. Redesign Onboarding Processes for Inclusion

    - **Coaching Opportunity:** Partner with HR, Functional leaders or Hiring Managers, to assess their onboarding processes and help them integrate a networking strategy into the process.
    - **Reflection Prompt:** Ask, "How does your current onboarding process help employees feel connected and valued from day one? What's missing?"

3. Recognize and Leverage Informal Networks

    - **Coaching Opportunity:** Consider using tools like Organizational Network Analysis (ONA) to help with career and leadership transitions and identify where critical connections may be missing.
    - **Reflection Prompt:** Ask leaders, "What is this data telling us? "Who in your team might be excluded from decision-making? What can you do to bring them in?"

4. Embed Inclusive Listening Practices

    - **Coaching Opportunity:** Introduce techniques like Nancy Kline's Thinking Environment into coaching sessions. Help leaders practice inclusive listening behaviors and adapt meeting protocols to be more inclusive.
    - **Reflection Prompt:** Ask leaders, "When you listen, are you focused on their perspective, or are you preparing your response? How can you create space for others to think and share more freely?"

5. Rethink Talent Development and Promotion Practices

- **Coaching Opportunity:** Guide leaders in reviewing their organization's competency frameworks and promotion criteria. Challenge them to question if these frameworks, do they genuinely identify and support diverse talent.
- **Reflection Prompt:** Ask, "How are we defining successful leadership here? Do our talent systems include different leadership styles?"

6. **Create Feedback Loops**

- **Coaching Opportunity:** Help leaders implement mechanisms for gathering and acting on feedback at one-to-one meetings or with small group meetings using the principles of the Thinking Environment.
- **Reflection Prompt:** Encourage reflection with questions, 'how do you encourage constructive dialogue across different stakeholder groups? Do others see you doing this?

Inclusion begins with a willingness to really see others, not just their roles or results, but their unique strengths, experiences, and humanity. Through Kline's Listening Practice, we saw how Weil's ideas of *attention and generosity* came to life. Using Kline's generative listening, this practice inspired one organization to embrace a new leadership style and redefine talent management.

In the next chapter, we look into mid to late career professionals, an overlooked aspect of inclusion: Career patterns and growth are critical in building an inclusive workplace, yet discussions around navigating and curating one's career seldom happen in any meaningful way. This gap is one of the biggest talent drains and a missed opportunity to address the global talent shortage. We show how having meaningful career conversations on a regular basis with all employees, whether newly joined or tenured, demonstrates inclusion. By doing this consistently, organizations naturally strengthen retention and engagement.

References

Carboni, I., Parker, A., & Langowitz, N. S. (2021). Mapping exclusion in the organization. MIT Sloan Management Review. https://sloanreview.mit.edu/article/mapping-exclusion-in-the-organization/

Deloitte. (2015). *The role of diversity practices and inclusion in promoting trust and employee engagement*. Deloitte Australia. https://www.deloitte.com/au/en/services/consulting/perspectives/role-diversity-practices-inclusion-trust-employee-engagement.html

Gallup. (2023, June 13). *The $8.8 trillion workplace problem: Gallup's State of the Global Workplace 2023 report*. https://www.gallup.com/workplace/393497/world-trillion-workplace-problem.aspx

Helgesen, S. (2023). *Rising together: How we can bridge divides and create a more inclusive workplace*. Hachette Go.

Kline, N. (1999). *Time to think: Listening to ignite the human mind*. Cassell.

Kline, N. (2009). More time to think: A way of being in the world. Fisher King Publishing.

Kouzes, J. M., & Posner, B. Z. (1987). *The leadership challenge: How to get extraordinary things done in organizations*. Jossey-Bass.

Maister, D. H., Green, C. H., & Galford, R. M. (2000). The trusted advisor. Free Press.

Raval, A. (2024, October 24). *Too many women excel at their jobs but are ignored for top roles*. Financial Times. https://www.ft.com/content/729d1a32-62bf-4d61-b3e3-0763b7fe93ca.

Tofade T, Elsner J, Haines ST. Best practice strategies for effective use of questions as a teaching tool. Am J Pharm Educ. 2013 Sep 12;77(7):155. https://doi.org/10.5688/ajpe777155. PMID: 24052658; PMCID: PMC3776909.

Woolsey, M. (2024, July 5). Want to keep staff on side? It's not rocket science. The Times. Retrieved from https://www.thetimes.com/business-money/companies/article/want-to-keep-staff-on-side-its-not-rocket-science-zvtgnf0hx

CHAPTER 7

Supporting Mid-to Late Career Professionals

Careers are Developed One Conversation at a Time.... Over Time
Beverly Kaye

A career conversation is usually thought of as fairly straightforward. Hard to misinterpret the two words: a conversation about your own career, or a meeting to let a team member know how they're doing overall. A career conversation can uncover what what's exciting about a particular role, a person's goals, and the next steps in a career path. An engaging and non-invasive talk to work with each other. At least, that's the assumption.

Does it ever happen that way? Despite being a powerful driver of engagement, these conversations, formal or informal, seem to be missing from the hallways and coffee bars inside organizations. And even more peculiar, managers, H.R. professionals and business leaders still thinks they're happening.

When I ask HR leaders about their career programs, here's what I usually hear:

Oh, we're really good at that... it's what we do.... It's who we are.

Or:

We just won the 'Best Employer' Award, so we know how to do this extremely well.

Not surprisingly, many employees have an appreciably different view. 40% of employees globally quit their jobs because of a lack of career progression (McKinsey et al. 2023) In Singapore the Institute of Management Accountants (IMA 2022), indicated that 50% of accounting and finance professionals intended to leave within a year due to a lack of career progression, feeling disengaged with their workplace.

It's always interesting when companies win 'best employer' awards, yet so many employees feel their career paths are unclear and few are having real career conversations. Maybe career conversations are not part of the criteria?

To better understand how missing career conversations affect employees, I coached mid-career professionals at a global technology firm who were experiencing these challenges. The following four stories show how reflective questions, and a structured approach broadened their thinking about roles and opened up new possibilities.

Bringing Career Conversations to Life

Mark: Redefining Success and Shifting Careers

One of my early sessions was with Mark, an engineer based in Singapore who had been with the company for 25 years. He had built his career working on complex technical systems, but the past few years he had become increasingly fascinated by the firm's AI initiatives He wanted to transition into AI yet wasn't sure how to make the leap without leaving his engineering roots behind.

As we started, I asked, "How do you define career success?" He paused before answering. *"I always thought success was about mastering my field, but now I think it's about adapting, staying ahead and contributing to something bigger."* it soon became clear that mentoring was a big part of his work. He had quietly guided younger engineers for years, shaping their technical expertise and problem-solving approaches. When I pointed this out, he laughed and said, *"I guess I've always been doing that without realizing it."*

His challenge wasn't a lack of skills but rather how to apply his experience in a new area. The firm had a policy whereby employees could apply for internal roles freely, but the unstructured nature of this process left him feeling lost. He worried: *How do I translate 25 years of engineering into something AI-focused?*

In our coaching, we identified his transferable skills: his comprehensive understanding of systems, his mentorship experience, and ability to troubleshoot complex problems. We also examined targeted ways he could get involved in AI projects before making a full transition.

When I asked, "Who else would you like to have in your network as a thought partner for your career?" which shifted his thinking. Rather than trying to jump into AI alone, he started to map out an internal and external network in the firm's AI initiatives. Mark realized he didn't need to start from scratch but could position himself as a bridge between engineering and AI.

Chris: Reframing Expertise to Create New Opportunities

Chris was a highly respected lawyer who'd been with the firm 20 years. She loved the company but felt stuck. She assumed the only path to advancement was to move abroad, yet personal commitments made relocation impossible.

During our conversation, I asked, *"Looking back, what's been your greatest career achievement?"* Without hesitation, she spoke about her early career in government advisory. She recalled how much she enjoyed that work but hadn't considered it relevant to her current role.

I followed up, *"If you left the firm tomorrow, what would you regret not doing?"*

She paused and said, *"I think I'd regret not using that experience in a bigger way. There's a real need for it here."*

As we thought more about this, she mentioned that one of her previous bosses in the US, who was about to retire, had encouraged her to move in that direction, adding her government advisory expertise into her current role. He firmly believed the organization needed this expertise more than ever and that her expertise would provide long-term strategic value.

At first, she dismissed the idea. *"I'm not sure that's even possible."* But as we worked through the possibilities, she began to see how she could reposition this experience and how it would add value to the firm.

In our coaching conversations, she reframed her career path, not as a lawyer in Asia but as an expert in government advisory with a global impact. She crafted a proposal to formally integrate this work into her role, pitched the idea to his boss, and they both presented to the global team. It offered Chris not only the advancement but fulfillment in her role without the need to exit the company. Like Mark, she was also a natural mentor to help new lawyers navigate the firm.

Marco: Redefining Strengths and Shifting Perceptions

Marco was a product marketing leader, another long-time employee of more than two decades, having moved from Italy to Spain to Texas. He was always seen as a high-potential employee, but only through the lens of his bosses. He had a few through the years and all saw him as an expert problem solver. His current boss relied on him as a troubleshooter, moving him around to fix struggling markets. While Marco appreciated the trust, he wanted something different.

I asked, *"How would you describe your strengths?"*

He listed a few technical skills, but when I probed further, he admitted, *"I've always been able to turn things around in tough markets. But I don't want to keep doing the same thing. I want to lead a bigger strategy, not just firefighting."*

His biggest challenge? His boss wasn't open to career conversations. Every time Marco tried to discuss his future; the response was *"You're too good at what you do."*

Through coaching, Marco realized that waiting for his boss to create opportunities wasn't an option. Initiating the conversation felt just as daunting. Since his boss saw him as the go-to person, Marco feared that pushing for something new might be perceived as abandoning his responsibilities or disrupting the team's stability.

At first, he wasn't sure how to start the conversation without sounding like he was signaling that he wanted to leave. Together, we worked on framing his request in a way that connected with his career goals and his boss's priorities:

Tying his request to business impact made more sense than talking about getting more visibility. Marco's angle was *"Attending leadership meetings would give us both a better understanding of how the other team thinks, what their pain points are, and how we can solve them."*

Even with this preparation, the conversation wasn't easy. His boss hesitated, but as they talked it through, he began to see the benefits and even suggested that Marco join a global team working on a high-visibility project.

Elena: Leading Remotely and Expanding Networks

Elena had built an impressive career over the decades across Russia, Germany, and Spain, moving across cultures and business units. She was now leading a remote team in Europe, and while she thrived on new challenges, she had reservations about keeping her team motivated from a distance.

I asked, "*What gives you energy in your job?*"

She replied that *"Building relationships, solving tough product challenges, and seeing my team succeed definitely energizes me."*

Her challenge wasn't just about remote leadership, it was about finding the right ways to stay energized and engaged. We worked on inclusive leadership strategies that fit her remote context. She realized that her ability to connect across markets and cultures was a core strength.

Another question that resonated with her was "*What strengths do you see in others that you'd like to develop?*" She admired leaders who built strong global networks. This led her to become more intentional about networking, making it a weekly priority rather than an afterthought. She started reaching out to peers in different regions, exchanging ideas, and learning from their approaches. One of these conversations led to a cross-functional collaboration, introducing her to a new team and a role she hadn't previously considered.

Questions That Made the Difference

Each of these professionals wanted to stay with the global tech firm. It wasn't about a promotion, more power, prestige or more compensation; they wanted to extend their careers.

These questions helped unlock that insight:

- *How would you define career success?*
- *Who else would you like to have in your network as a thought partner for your career?*
- *Looking back, what have been your greatest career achievements?*
- *If you left the company today, what would you regret not having done?*
- *What gives you energy in your job?*
- *What strengths do you see in others that you'd like to develop?*
- *How would you describe your strengths?*

We also asked:

- *If you could never fail, what career would you explore?*
- *What are you looking forward to this year?*
- *If you were to teach, what subject would that be?*
- *What assumptions might be getting in the way of that conversation (with your boss or with another function?)*

Beyond the impact on individuals, these conversations uncovered new capabilities within the organization. By anonymously consolidating this data, we provided the firm with a clearer picture of its internal talent marketplace, helping the leadership team recognize untapped internal expertise. This broader organizational perspective reinforced the value and advantage of ongoing career conversations.

We used structured questions and an adaptive coaching approach, one that balanced listening with reflective questions. While each session lasted 60 minutes, the focus wasn't on directing employees toward a predefined path but on creating space for them to reflect on their career story in their own way. This approach helped employees get insights they hadn't considered, making the conversation both structured and fluid.

An Adaptive Career Coaching Approach: Preparing Without Over-Structuring

Coaching is not about having the answers, it's creating the conditions for insights to emerge. As Tim Gallwey suggests in The Inner Game of Work, real learning and growth happen when we remove interference and allow those insights to surface. Similarly, Ginny Whitelaw, in The Zen Leader emphasizes shifting from control to connection, something essential in coaching when the real work is about holding space, not directing outcomes.

With this in mind, the following approach helps balance preparation with generative listening. Preparation is essential, but the substantive work happens in the space between questions, in the pauses, and in the unexpected turns a conversation takes.

Step 1: Frame the Conversation with Curiosity.

Before the session, write down possible questions to explore the coachee's situation. Consider:

- What uncertainties might they be facing?
- What assumptions might they be holding onto?
- What do they need clarity on?
  (It's not about following a checklist; it's about listening for what matters.)

Step 2: Ask and Create Space for Thought

Start with a simple, open-ended question. Then pause. I mean *really* pause.

- Give the coachee time to process.
- If they respond quickly ask, "Is there more, you would like to say?"
- Sometimes the richest insights come from the response after the second question.

Step 3: Return to the Core Challenge

As the conversation unfolds, circle back the core career dilemma or opportunity:

- "The real challenge is... [insert their words]. Does that feel accurate to you?"
- You're not leading; you're helping them see their own patterns.

For example, in Mark's case, it might be:

- *"It sounds like moving into AI is part of your goal, but the real challenge might be that your current network still sees you as an engineer, and your boss continues to view you as a technical expert rather than a broader contributor in AI. Does that feel right to you?"*

- *"What would it take for others to start seeing your potential in AI? Could expanding your network be part of that shift?"*

Step 4: Follow the Emerging Themes

As you listen, new patterns will start to take shape.

- Rather than rushing to a solution, stay with the theme and unpack it.
- Use reflective restating: "So what I'm hearing is…"
- Ask the coachee if this is the right area to investigate further.

Step 5: Hold Space for Insight

This is where *The Thinking Environment* approach comes in:

- Ask: *"What more do you want to think or say about this?"*
- Step back, let go of your own need to guide, and trust the coachee's own wisdom to surface.

WHY CAREER CONVERSATIONS ARE STILL MISSING

Despite the power of reflective coaching, real career conversations remain rare inside organizations. Why is that? Having coached hundreds of managers on career conversations, I have some thoughts. I was curious to better understand their experiences, whether they had meaningful career discussions with their own bosses. Some said yes but the majority said no. If career conversations are so essential to both employee and employer, why such a perception gap?

Their responses echoed what Dr. Beverly Kaye found in her research on careers and employee engagement. In her book *Help Them Grow or Watch Them Go*, she identified fears and myths that hold managers back from having these conversations.

The most common myth is a lack of time, and I've also found that time, (or the perceived lack of it) is a convenient excuse for almost everything in one's daily life: *I'll write a book, I'll get going to the gym, I'll make time build my network and* so forth. *I'll get to it soon.*

The added difference is not simply making the time for oneself, but making time for another person, which is also the hallmark of management. Perhaps that's the fear.

Beyond excuses for time, I uncovered even bigger concerns, particularly during a corporate restructuring. Kaye also highlights four common challenges that prevent managers from engaging in career conversations:

1. "If I don't talk about it, they may not think about it..."
2. "Since employees need to own their careers, it's not my job."
3. "Everyone wants more money, bigger or better; promotions, raises, prestige, and power."
4. "Development efforts are best concentrated on high potentials."

All of this sounds familiar, but that last point stood out for me. I've heard many variations on that line that is even more concerning for inclusion:

'We only invest in early careers rather than late-career professionals.' And yes, I assure you I've heard that comment repeatedly over the years. It's not simply about age bias, but a limitation of opportunities for experienced employees who are still on their game.

Not a myth. A bias.

I also have heard managers question whether an employee nearing retirement should even be considered for promotion, casual comments made openly without asking what the employee may want in their career path. Another angle I've seen is to use proximity to retirement as a justification for not promoting candidates, with a rhetorical flourish of "why invest in someone who's only a few years shy of retirement?"

At one financial institution, I was told outright:

We don't hire anyone over 45.

As that seemed rather young, I asked why. The response was:

They just don't have the energy and are usually reluctant to learn a new system.

Such statements aren't factual, obviously. They're untested assumptions that excludes qualified professionals from an ongoing career path. Poking a bit more, I replied

> *So, just curious. Do you think it's true that people start losing their brain cells after 45?*

The room went silent. But the bias comment lingered and for some, no doubt, it stung.

The managers I interviewed shared those same four reasons from Kaye's (2024) book, adding that they often were uncomfortable facilitating such discussions. They felt that career conversations tend to be unstructured or counterproductive without the right skills and approach. While there is a clear link between ongoing career dialogues and improved engagement, the question then becomes: how do we encourage managers to interact more actively and confidently?

This isn't just hype; it's based on my observations with clients and quantifiable data from Gallup, Harvard Business Review, and LinkedIn Talent Solutions. Right Management Survey states 82% of employees stated they would feel more engaged if their managers held regular career conversations with them. The evidence is consistent: employees who have ongoing career conversations with their managers were far more likely to stay put.

When I coached a group of mid-career professionals at a global tech firm, I observed its impact. One of the most important managements 'ingredients' is knowing how to ask the right questions. So when a question, positioned properly, sparked reflection or offered clarity, it reinforced commitment.

The question, therefore, must move beyond the anodyne "in the next few years where do you see yourself?' and towards helping people reconnect with values, strengths and the impact they want to make. These questions get to the heart of what people want. Questions like what's one value you won't compromise? What gives you energy in your current role? How would you define your unique strength and how does this impact the firm?

Beyond the Conversation: Bias, Ageism, and Missed Opportunities

I still see far too many mid-career professionals experience subtle biases that limit their opportunities. In Asia the discussions around workplace inclusion are increasingly focused on ageism.

The absence of career conversations disproportionately impacts mid-career professionals, the ones (mentioned above) who are overlooked or not considered for opportunities. This breeds disengagement and goes beyond individual frustration to company morale and workplace inclusion.

Some organizations do value tenure, but others encourage the churn, many times through the prism of age bias, rather than availing themselves of expertise.

For some industries experience isn't just valued, it's critical to sustaining the organisations. Disney for example, places significant value on its Imagineers, recognizing the depth of creativity and technical expertise they bring, particularly when building the parks in Hong Kong and Shanghai.

Many academic institutions use the knowledge of emeritus professors, involving them in ongoing research, mentoring, and advisory roles well beyond retirement. In the world's Blue Zones, regions known for longevity, doctors continue practicing well beyond traditional retirement age. In business, leaders like Charlie Munger, Warren Buffett, and Li Ka-shing remained active and influential into their 90s, proving that experience is irreplaceable.

Countries like Singapore, Japan, and China face some of the world's fastest aging and declining populations and are at the forefront of these discussions. In response to such challenges, some countries have revised mandatory retirement policies to encourage the hiring and retention of experienced professionals. Policies cannot change a mindset, and biases continue to limit careers for tenured employees. The following chart illustrates recent shifts in retirement policies across several Asia-Pacific countries, reflecting an ongoing effort to encourage workforce participation.

Changes in Mandatory Retirement Age Across Asia

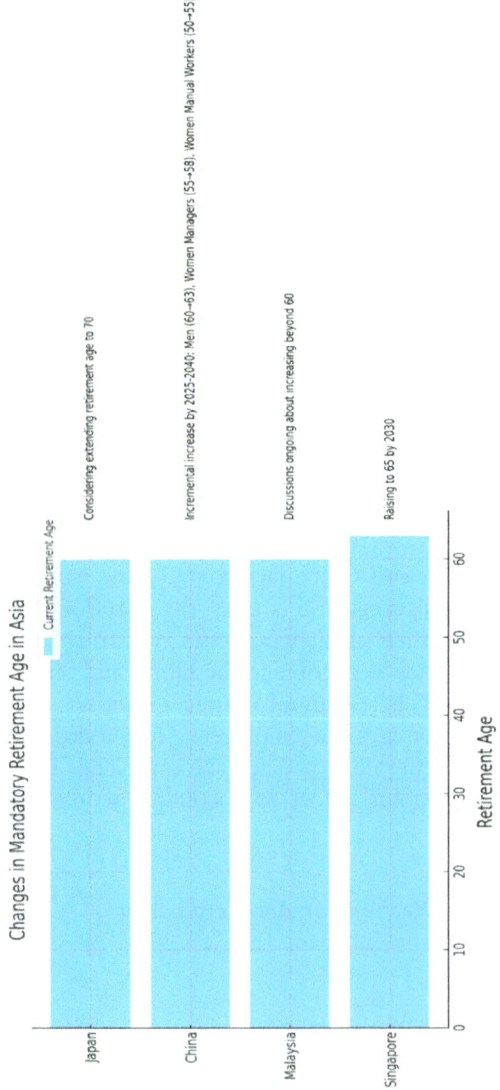

The 'Age 35 Phenomenon' and Its Impact on Career Advancement

In Asia, demographics show how quickly the region is changing. China's population in 2020 was roughly 20% age 60 and above. But unlike other aging economies, age discrimination in China begins much earlier, a trend known as the *"age 35 phenomenon."*

China's retirement policies are evolving, but ageism remains ingrained in the private and public sectors. Civil service job postings explicitly state that applicants must be under 35 (National Civil Service Administration 2020) which only reinforce this reality. Such a government mandated hiring requirement sets a precedent that ripples through the corporate world, where younger candidates are overwhelmingly preferred. China has recently reformed its retirement policy, starting in 2025. For men, the retirement age will increase from 60 to 63 over 15 years. For women in managerial positions, it will rise from 55 to 58.

Companies known for their inclusion and diversity practices aren't immune to age-related bias. Google settled an age discrimination lawsuit in 2019, agreeing to a multi-million-dollar payout to over 200 job seekers over 40 who alleged they were passed over despite their relevant experience. IBM faced similar scrutiny when they laid off nearly 20,000 U.S. employees over 40, about 60% of its total job cuts. As Bloomberg reported, internal emails revealed IBM executives referring to older workers as *"dinobabies"* and suggesting they should become an *"extinct species."*

Age discrimination doesn't appear in job ads as boldly as it did in the 1950s but is still visible, just more subtly. Finding an image of someone over 50 on any corporate career site takes effort. The ugly truth is that ageism remains alive and unlike other biases, it's tolerated.

It's Worse for Mid-Career Women

The impact of ageism is even more severe for women. A 2024 women in media report found that 35% of women in mid-and-senior career position were considering quitting and 56% had a negative view of their career progression, signaling widespread disengagement.

A survey by the Social Investigation Center of China Youth Daily revealed that 86% of nearly 2000 white-collar professionals believe career opportunities decline sharply for women after 30 a noticeably younger threshold compared to similar perceptions in countries like the U.S. or the U.K., where age-related career barriers are often noted later. What's worse is many leave the workforce before reaching management roles, only to find that returning is nearly impossible. While some initiatives aim to reintegrate older employees, systemic ageism remains a significant barrier. Policy changes alone are not enough to shift entrenched workplace attitudes. The World Bank highlights that despite China's retirement age for women increasing from 50 to 58, structural barriers continue to limit their re-entry into the workforce.

In the United States, 30% of women aged 50 and above report experiencing age-related discrimination. The ILO women's labor force participation stands at 47%, with 37% in Asia, and an impressive 72% in Vietnam. However, the UN highlights as women progress in their careers, their representation in management and decision-making roles decreases. For instance, in 2022, women held only 28% of managerial positions worldwide. This data underscores the structural barriers and outdated mindsets impacting women's career advancement. It's not merely a matter of personal choice or entrepreneurial pursuits; ingrained systems and biases have not evolved in tandem with the changing workforce demographics. Addressing these gaps is not optional but essential for sustaining the workforce. But inclusion doesn't happen spontaneously; it requires conviction, commitment, and a fundamental shift in behaviours.

My research highlights this disconnect. While organizations claim to embrace inclusion, many fail to address the structural and cultural barriers that exclude experienced professionals from career conversations. Age bias is rarely called out as explicitly, compared to other forms of discrimination, (as I mentioned earlier in this chapter), but its impact is as significant. Jo Ann Jenkins, CEO of AARP shares in her book Disrupt Aging "The negative stereotypes of aging are so ingrained in our society and personal identities, they are difficult to overcome." It's not an American issue, it's global. Older workers are not only overlooked but pushed aside before they're ready to leave, despite their skills, knowledge, and contributions.

Why This Matters

Start with the demographics. As of 2020, 37% of the global workforce was aged 50 and over. By 2050, that figure will rise on average to 45% across OECD countries. Despite the fact that older workers making up a growing share of the labor market, they still struggle to find jobs, stay employed, and earn promotions. With China's shrinking population and an aging workforce, how long can a preference for young candidates last? The math doesn't add up. As the talent pool of 35-year-olds diminishes, organizations will have no choice but to rethink outdated hiring practices and tap into the experience of mid- and late-career professionals. Whether they can do so in time is the pressing question.

This is where inclusion and economics overlap. Addressing ageism goes beyond fairness, it's an economic imperative. In Japan, Singapore and the U.S., workforce demographics are shifting rapidly. With fewer younger people entering the job market, companies that fail to retain experienced employees will face skill shortages. Many older professionals want to continue working, contributing their expertise while remaining productive members of society. Organizations that recognize and act on these changes by creating bridges of inclusive career paths will have a competitive talent advantage.

Mid-to-late career professionals (typically those over 45) are at the heart of workplace culture, yet many feel invisible. Despite their expertise, their true value lies in their holistic understanding of how the organization operates and their ability to mentor others. However, career development opportunities often favor younger employees, leaving this group undervalued and underutilized.

Rather than being sidelined, they should be actively engaged. Investing in experienced employees, including mid-to-late career professionals, has been shown to drive performance. A study by Forrester Consulting found that companies prioritizing employee experience achieved 1.7 times faster revenue growth and 2.3 times greater customer lifetime value than other firms.

Addressing these issues is not only a matter of equity but also a strategic business decision. By creating an inclusive environment that values the experience of mid-to-late career professionals, organizations drive performance and adapt to evolving market dynamics.

Given the demographic shifts in Asia, it's time to revamp career development and embrace lifelong employability, offering careers that help all employees contribute, stay relevant, and remain engaged.

Three Action Steps

The first step is to simply acknowledge ageism. I found most people don't realize when they're part of the problem. Comments like "they're just low on energy" or "we don't hire anyone over 45" may seem harmless, but by taking the time to pause, they expose entrenched biases that exclude others.

The second step is including mid-career and older employees in career conversations. Amplifying inclusion in diversity initiatives; creating a workplace where everyone, regardless of age, is part of the conversation.

The third step is acknowledging that a single career conversation a year isn't enough. Career development isn't a check-the-box exercise, it's an ongoing dialogue that supports employees at every career stage Beverly Kaye writes that a career conversation's goal is to help people grow. I'd add that it is also about helping people uncover who they are and where they want to go.

The most powerful tool that organizations have at their disposal to build an inclusive work environment is an ongoing career conversation. From my work in factories in the Philippines, the financial sector global entertainment companies in the Asia Pacific Region, I've seen how short, regular career conversations drive real engagement. When managers take the time to have meaningful discussions to help employees find purpose at work, there is almost always a renewed commitment to their role.

Imagine that every employee in your company has career conversations, not about 'what's my next role,' but about what energizes them on their way to work, what makes them stay, and how they want to contribute. Flip the narrative. Employees at all stages of their careers are already having career conversations, but too often, those discussions happen with recruiters instead of their own leaders. If leaders don't create space for these conversations, someone else will.

The Path Forward

In this chapter, we explored career stories from mid-career professionals at a global technology company that recognized the need to better support experienced employees. Using structured conversations and reflective questions drawn from my book, *Now It's Clear: The Career You Own*, we saw how expanding thinking about roles and possibilities helped individuals reconnect with their strengths and next steps. When career conversations are a regular part of the workplace, organizations unlock the full potential of their people. Engagement rises and inclusion becomes a reality, not an ideal. I'm optimistic that if organizations move beyond annual performance reviews to ongoing career conversations, we'll see an uptick in productivity and performance. A thoughtful conversation can create lasting impact and enhance inclusion.

If career conversations can create such an impact, what would happen if a company scaled them across the organization? In the next section, we look at how one company turned these ideas into action.

WHAT ONE GLOBAL TECH COMPANY GOT RIGHT ABOUT CAREER CONVERSATIONS

Through my work across Asia Pacific, I've helped organizations find ways to mitigate bias, specifically ageism. One time, a Fortune 100 global technology company with over 50,000 employees worldwide, known for its leadership in IT services asked me to assist a group of highly technical, mid-career to later professionals who needed guidance on their career steps.

Rather than a structured program, this firm wanted something quite different, a 90-minutes master class on career navigation, followed by individual career coaching sessions. We became the firm's internal career coaches. Initially, we focused on mid-career technical experts, but over time the coaching sessions included a broader group of employees. What was driving this program was the firm's strong reputation for employee development. However, like other clients, they found that mid-to-late career professionals were not included in these programs and were missing critical career conversations. Surveys confirmed this gap, when asked about development opportunities, a significant portion of these employees responded negatively, which was directly linked to a noticeable drop in morale.

The results?

- Increased engagement
- Greater participation in the firm's network groups
- A rise in informal mentoring circles
- Renewed sense of purpose

Through Zoom, we facilitated interactive sessions across Asia, Europe, and North America, encouraging participants to take greater ownership of their careers and emphasizing the value of informal networks. Rekindling connections across the firm often made a difference between feeling stuck and discovering new organizational possibilities. The next step was to reconnect with others to open new doors within the company.

We started a 90-minutes Masterclass, designed to get people thinking about what's next and how to actually see existing opportunities within the firm. The Masterclass and coaching sessions were directly linked to the company's career pathing program, helping employees rethink their careers instead of plateauing.

The firm encouraged participants to sign up for individual coaching, knowing this would help turn insights into action. While the Masterclass expanded their thinking, the one-on-one coaching conversations gave them space to use these insights.

In the first round of coaching, I worked with over 20 professionals at a career crossroads. Most were unsure about their next step, while others felt stuck in their roles and unsure if they could actually move ahead, so our conversations looked at options and ownership.

I've discussed this idea of *career ownership* with other clients and in my book, *Now It's Clear*, where I outlined a framework to help mid to late career professionals find clarity and purpose. Through coaching, we applied this approach to guide people to take stock of who they are and develop strategies to act on these insights.

Whether in person or on Zoom, there are few better ways to witness an employee's shift than meeting face-to-face. One of the most powerful aspects of these coaching sessions was to see each person's unique career. Listening to their stories, some were actively seeking new opportunities, others grappling with uncertainty and questioning their next steps, others rediscovering their purpose within the firm.

Final Thought: Letting Go and Coaching Through Listening

Great coaching doesn't follow a script, it's about creating space to see what emerges and unfolds. It requires a balance of preparation and an ability to let go, listen, and respond to what is in the moment. The best coaches don't force a direction; they cultivate an environment where the coachee discovers his or her own path forward.

While coaching mid to late career professionals is about helping individuals gain clarity and take ownership of their careers, the conversations become more complex when career decisions involve two people. In the next chapter, we uncover the complexities faced by dual-career couples who both have jobs and pursue their respective careers.

Dual-career couples reflect a fundamental change in workforce dynamics, with an estimated 60–70% of households balancing the realities of two careers (McKinsey 2019; UK Office for National Statistics 2022; U.S. Bureau of Labor Statistics 2024; Singapore Ministry of Manpower 2022; Permits Foundation 2022). This also signals the future of inclusion, as organizations rethink workplace structures, leadership models, and talent selection. In addition, they have an opportunity to broaden their talent pool by adopting a more holistic approach to mobility and career development, an approach already embraced by some multinationals like Nestlé, P&G, Maersk and others.

This is where a skillful coach, or someone with a background in family counseling can offer valuable support, helping both individuals and couples navigate career transitions successfully.

REFERENCES

Institute of Management Accountants. (2022). *Global perspectives on talent retention in the accounting and finance profession: Asia-Pacific focus*. https://web.iaiglobal.or.id/assets/files/file_berita/IMAGlobalTalentRetentionReport asiapacificFinal.pdf

Kaye, B., & Giulioni, J. W. (2024). *Help them grow or watch them go: Career conversations organizations need and employees still want* (3rd ed.). Berrett-Koehler Publishers.

McKinsey & Company. (2019, September 12). *How dual-career couples find fulfillment at work*. McKinsey & Company. https://www.mckinsey.com/capabilities/people-and-organizational-performance/our-insights/how-dual-career-couples-find-fulfillment-at-work

McKinsey & Company, & Lean In. (2023). *Women in the workplace 2023*. https://www.mckinsey.com/featured-insights/diversity-and-inclusion/women-in-the-workplace

Permits Foundation. (2022). *International dual careers survey report*. Retrieved from https://www.permitsfoundation.com/wp-content/uploads/2022/10/Oct_13_2022_Partner_Survey_Report_Final.pdf

Singapore: Ministry of Manpower, Singapore. (2022, January 28). *Labour Force in Singapore 2021.* https://stats.mom.gov.sg/Pages/Labour-Force-InSingapore-2021.aspx

UK: Office for National Statistics. (2022, July 22). *Families and the labour market*, UK: 2021. ONS. https://www.ons.gov.uk/employmentandlabourmarket/peopleinwork/employmentandemployeetypes/articles/familiesandthelabourmarketengland/2021/previous/v1

US: U.S. Bureau of Labor Statistics. (2024). *Employment projections: 2024–34 highlights.* U.S. Bureau of Labor Statistics. https://www.bls.gov/emp/

CHINA DATA: ENGLISH CITATION

National Civil Service Administration. (2020). Provisions on recruitment of civil servants. Retrieved from http://www.scs.gov.cn/zcfg/202001/t20200108_16198.html

CHAPTER 8

Inclusive Careers for Dual-Career Couples

The freedom to shape our lives is the most precious freedom we have.
Amartya Sen

The rise of dual-career couples, where both partners actively pursue professional roles, is a global trend across industries, from academia to NGOs. Importantly, I'm seeing a shift where women are driving international career moves, challenging the assumption that they are "trailing" partners. As women drive this shift, I'm hoping we see a change in definition, as 'I've never found 'trailing' to be a positive adjective, framing one partner as secondary as if they're walking wearily behind rather than actively shaping their career. Besides reconsidering the term, the demographics bode well for organizations offering a powerful opportunity to rethink talent mobility and better support dual-career families.

I receive an email on a regular basis, mostly from women in senior positions asking about dual-career challenges. The email starts with, "I've just received an incredible opportunity, my dream job in "X" city. Can we talk next week? I'm concerned. It's not me, it's my partner. What will happen to his/her career?"

The Asia Pacific head of product marketing for a global cosmetic brand (known for moving talent around the world) asked if I'd speak with one of her high-potential talents, Min Seo. This wasn't a formal coaching engagement she'd attended one of my talks on dual-career professionals and asked if I could have an informal conversation with Min Seo, who had been with the firm since college, worked across internal teams and now the head of digital marketing for their personal care business.

She had just been offered a promotion in China but for the first time wasn't sure if it was the right move. Her boss had said to me 'we don't want to lose her, but not sure what's holding her back. Could you talk to her?'

We met at a small local coffee shop near her office, the ceiling fan pushing humid air around the room. Min Seo ordered an iced coffee, took a sip and absentmindedly traced a circle on the condensation of the glass. We sat in silence for a short while and then she simply said, "I'm not sure about this move."

"Min Seo", I replied "you've moved across the world before. What's different this time?"

The story unfolded from there.

"It's not the move. It's not the travel. It's not the role. I know I can do the job. But for the past decade, we've moved for my career, and my partner (working for the same company) had to put his on hold. The firm always says they support dual-career couples, but so far, that's meant résumé help and introductions to search consultants. It's just not enough anymore."

She looked straight me.

"He needs a real opportunity now. Not networking, not vague guidance. No disrespect to career coaches, but this is different. We joined at the same time, and he's really talented and has more to offer the firm. I want to move and stay with them, but I just can't take this role unless they step up and offer some sort of solution."

"That makes sense. Curious, what would a meaningful solution look like for your partner?"

She paused longer than usual before answering.

"A real job opportunity. Something that fits his experience."

"If they made that effort, would you feel differently about taking the role?"

"Yes. But I need to know they're not just saying the right things. They have to follow through. Actually, they should talk to him about a role before I even consider this move."

"So, how do you want to approach that conversation with your boss? What feels like the best way to have this discussion?"

Since that discussion in 2017, dual-career coaching has become part of my practice. Min Seo took that conversation back to her boss, but change didn't happen overnight. She shared why she was reluctant to take on another role and asked the firm to reexamine its dual-career commitments. After several discussions, she accepted the role. Today, it's not uncommon for candidates and employees to negotiate support for their partners as part of a job offer or a promotion either through an introduction to the business community or a role within the partner's company.

As more women pursue career opportunities that involve relocation, they are increasingly asking: "What support do you offer for my partner?" Based on my research, I've observed a shift where not only women but also Millennials and Gen Z professionals, regardless of gender, are inquiring about how organizations support dual-career couples. This trend reflects broader changes in career expectations, mobility, and partnership dynamics pushing organisations to rethink policies.

Not long after my conversation with Min Seo, I heard from Vanna, the head of finance for a global food company, who found herself in a similar situation as Min Seo. Vanna had built a global career with the firm and had been offered a role in Switzerland. Her partner, meanwhile, had a great role in New York. On paper, it looked like an incredible opportunity. Yet when we spoke, her excitement was mixed with hesitation. She shared, "I've taken every opportunity the company has offered. But now, it's not just about me, it's about both of us." During our coaching conversations, it became clear that Vanna had never fully paused to consider what she wanted from her career or what a move would mean for both partners.

To help her navigate the decision, we used a structured tool called the Intelligent Career Card System (ICCS), designed to clarify career motivations and choices. I'll return to Vanna's story later in the chapter to show how career coaching with the ICCS process helped Vanna and her partner clarify what mattered most as they considered next steps.

Building on this, I introduce a holistic career planning approach, using coaching and the Intelligent Career Card System (ICCS), a structured tool designed for both individuals and dual-career couples. Through a case study of Vanna and her partner's planned move from the U.S. to Europe, we look at the challenges they identified and the solutions that supported their decision-making. Drawing on research and coaching practice, I show how the Intelligent Career Card System (ICCS) helped both partners assess their why, how, and whom for career navigation, adapting individual career planning to two independent career paths.

Navigating opportunity without sacrificing both partners' aspirations is a regular dilemma for dual-career couples. I first began working with this group in 2016 while researching diversity and inclusion policies at Hong Kong University. As part of a study for the Gender Studies Programme, I reviewed the policies of the top 30 universities globally and came across stories of dual-career professionals. Some universities had already started changing policies to support dual-career academics. Since then, I've continued to research how institutions and organizations are adapting to the evolving needs of dual-career couples.

Having spent the bulk of my career working for multinationals in the Asia Pacific Region I observed the challenges but also recognized opportunities for this particular group. As mentioned in the last chapter, career conversations are not always forthcoming for mid-to-late career professionals. Indeed, I would add that they've been non-existent for dual career couples. I've worked with internal and external mobility professionals to coordinate such moves, mostly tactical rather than strategic. Some organizations and governments have this down to a science, but many still do not grasp the complexities of dealing with two executives rather than one, which is where the challenge begins.

Compared to other sectors, academia is often further ahead with dual career policies, practices, programs and support, particularly due to early advocacy by women in STEM. Women physics PhDs led the charge, demanding institutional policies that supported their careers alongside their partners. In 1999, Physics Today shared the challenges faced by dual-career couples in physics, which they coined as the 'two-body problem', the difficulty of both partners obtaining jobs at the same university, a narrow specialty or within a reasonable commuting distance from each other.

For faculty, the dilemma of pursuing their career meant prolonged separation, straining the relationship, while choosing to stay together required one partner to put their research or career on hold.

These discussions created an avenue for institutions to develop policies for dual-career partners and in doing so, strengthened the retention of talented physicists, particularly women. Also in the 1990s universities began revising their dual-career policies to support academic couples. The University of Michigan started its Dual-Career Program in 1994, and Stanford University established the Dual-Career Assistance Program in

1998, with significant contributions from the Stanford Clayman Institute for Gender Research. Today, 36% of full-time faculty at leading U.S. universities have an academic partner, with higher rates among women (40%) than men (34%) (Schiebinger et al. 2008). As Londa Schiebinger of the Clayman Institute observed: *"Couples vote with their feet, leaving or not considering universities that don't support them."*

In Asia, those shifts began later and information about structured programs and policies varied considerably across institutions and countries. In 2015, Nagoya University in Japan supported international faculty through joint degree programs and research initiatives which indirectly benefited dual-career couples. In 2018, The Australian National University took a more structured approach with its "Dual Career Academic Couples" program, providing solutions to attract and retain academic couples and strengthening its position in global faculty recruitment.

In response to market changes, universities began updating policies to align with the evolving dynamics of academic careers. After I conducted this research, I recommended that other industries use these templates, that is, approach dual-career couples not as an accommodation but rather a talent source to fill the global talent shortage. From a global perspective, the rise of dual-career couples is hardly limited to academia. Businesses and NGOs are starting to view dual-career couples as an untapped resource that brings complementary experiences, diverse perspectives and a range of capabilities from their respective jobs and industries.

Despite growing awareness, hurdles remain. Definitions alone present a challenge. I mentioned that 'trailing spouse' is not viewed positively and that 'two-body problem' or 'two-fer' deal subtly reinforce bias against partners in dual career-relationships.

As Patty Sotirin and Sonia M. Goltz (2019) mention in their research, the *two-body problem,* when applied to academia and careers, suggests an inevitable, mechanistic tension between partners' professional trajectories. This metaphor is not neutral; it simplifies complex career negotiations and dehumanizes the individuals involved. Even when institutions offer dual hires, the assumption that one partner is an add-on, that *"two-fer deal",* diminishes individual merit. This type of language reinforces subtle yet persistent hierarchies, eroding the recognition of both partners as equally competent professionals.

In addition, institutional support remains inconsistent. Some universities offer dedicated staff, clear policies and funding to support partner hires, while others provide basic job search help or little formal resources, leaving dual career couples to navigate employment challenges independently. The same is true for multinationals and NGO's.

Why does this matter? Dual-career couples are here to stay, with Asia, Europe and the US increasing its percentage of dual career households:

- **Singapore:** In 2020, approximately 52.5% of married couples were dual-career earners (Singstat)
- **Japan**: The labor force participation rate for women reached 71.3% in 2020, in 2023, approximately 12.8 million households in Japan were dual-income statista.com
- **United States**: In 2021, approximately 60% of married couples were dual earners, reflecting a significant increase from previous decades. (OECD)
- **European Union**: In 2020, about 65% of couples were dual earners (OECD)

There are differences within each country or region but overall, the data shows an upward trend of dual-income households, influenced by evolving gender roles and economic factors. This represents a significant but underutilized source of talent with diverse capabilities and despite the inconsistencies mentioned above, organizations can learn from academia's leadership, adopt inclusive policies, and rethink talent mobility. In doing so, they can unlock a highly skilled talent pool ready to thrive in the global workforce.

To understand the real impact of these challenges, I spoke with men and women navigating career choices while researching dual careers, typically when couples were deciding on a role in another country. The one overarching theme was the challenge of balancing professional opportunities for both partners, even more pronounced for younger professionals. An EY study found that 78% of Millennials have a partner working full-time and expect dual-career support. Similarly, additional research on Millennial professionals showed that dual careers are the new norm. Companies risk losing top talent if they fail to address these needs.

I continue to hear such stories, particularly among women. The Permits Foundation's International Dual Careers Survey Report (2022) surveyed 730 expatriate spouses, revealing that over 75% would not move to a country where their partner faced work permit restrictions. Additionally, 26% of respondents considered leaving their host country due to limited work access. The study noted a significant rise in expectations for partner employment support since 2008, a period marked by the global financial crisis (Great Recession), after which dual-income households increasingly became an economic necessity and priority for expatriate families.

The Permits Foundation's report refers to 'spouses' broadly, so we can't assume whether this response skews more toward men or women. In my work, most of the leaders who reach out to me with these concerns are women. This could be reflective of broader gender dynamics, where women, having historically adapted their careers for their partners, now find themselves negotiating for dual-career support in ways that men may not have had to in previous generations. That said, I've also heard similar concerns from younger male leaders, particularly among Millennials where dual-career decision-making is becoming more balanced.

This shift requires more than just policy changes within organizations. it calls for external reforms, such as lobbying governments for visa policies changes which directly impact talent mobility. Without any meaningful change, companies risk losing skilled talent.

Visa challenges vary by country, creating additional barriers for dual-career families: (MOFA 2022; USCIS 2023; European Commission 2022).

- **Japan**: Dependent visas often prohibit full-time work.
- **U.S.**: H-4 visa holders face changing employment policies.
- **Europe**: Support focuses on local integration rather than immediate work permits.

In contrast, countries like Canada, Australia, and Singapore have more progressive policies, such as open work permits for skilled workers' spouses, making them more attractive destinations for global talent.

While these policies are essential for global talent mobility, organizations need to move beyond compliance and think strategically about the next generation of leaders. Dual-career professionals represent a valuable talent pool, that should be included into leadership discussions, talent management planning, and mobility strategies.

At present, some organizations remain ill-equipped to navigate the complexities of dual-career talent. A more forward-thinking approach is to borrow best practices from academic institutions, which have established partner hiring strategies that can help companies tailor solutions to their needs. Organizations that take both a tactical approach to address visa challenges and a strategic approach to recognizing dual-career professionals as part of their talent segment will not only enhance inclusion but also strengthen their position as an employer of choice in an increasingly competitive talent landscape.

In my coaching experience, most organizations may have some policies in place (though often loosely defined) but almost all of them lack the career tools and mindset needed to support dual-career couples. Organizations that build this capability to recognize career success as a shared journey will better position themselves for the future. By doing so, they reflect a greater sense of inclusion and humanity within their culture.

INCLUSIVE CAREERS, GLOBAL MOBILITY AND ORGANISATIONAL SUPPORT

Dual-career support is more than just an HR benefit. It is an inclusive strategy that builds equity in career opportunities while strengthening organizational talent pipelines. Some organizations (listed below) recognize the value of supporting dual-career couples, particularly in a global workforce, as it contributes to attracting and retaining talent in a mutually beneficial way for both firm and employee.

In 2011, Nestle co-founded the International Dual Career Network (IDCN), a global non-profit association in Switzerland to support the professional integration of partners and spouses of relocating employees. IDCN is now in 15 locations worldwide, collaborating with over 120 corporate members, multinationals, NGOs and academic institutions. Below are examples across corporate, academic, and NGO sectors, showing how dual-career support is gaining momentum worldwide.

Corporate

- **Procter & Gamble (P&G):** Partners with the International Dual Career Network (IDCN) to offer job and networking support for spouses.

- **General Electric (GE) and PwC:** Provide career transition services for expatriate partners.
- **Nestlé:** Leads a global initiative helping partners of relocating employees find jobs through career support, networking, and HR access. Through its Spouse Career Centre Partnership since 2008, it has provided job market guidance and networking support for employees' spouses in Switzerland.
- **Maersk Diversity & Inclusion Initiatives:** Focus on flexible work policies and inclusive hiring, indirectly supporting dual-career couples. Professional Development Programs offer training and mentorship, enabling adaptable career paths for employees and their partners.
- **Deloitte:** Supports dual-career couples through flexible career programs like Skills First Professionals for non-traditional paths and initiatives for workforce re-entry. They also advocate for partner employment rights through the Permits Foundation and offer roles to help individuals balance dual careers effectively.
- **In Asia,** change is underway as women's participation rises. Japan's Nadeshiko Brands promote women's career advancement and co-parenting. Sysmex Corporation has been recognized for creating a workplace that supports dual-career and co-parenting employees.
- Arvato Systems (Malaysia and India) offers a dual career model with both management and expert career tracks.
- **IDCN Member Companies in Asia Pacific:** Provide dual-career support across the region.

Academic Institutions

- **Several Europe** universities emphasize local employment support. The **University of Copenhagen** offers career counseling and subsidized work opportunities for partners, while **ETH Zurich** in Switzerland has supported dual-career faculty since 1999.
- **Keio University and University of Tsukuba** are taking early steps to support dual-career couples.

NGOs
- **The Asian Development Bank (ADB)**: Published research on dual-career couples, provides career-related support for spouses and domestic partners, helps with opportunities in the Philippines or across the region through a standard recruitment process, and recognizes the challenges with visa regulations in the Philippines

While these organizational practices are important, the missing link for dual-career success is making career decisions. Tools like the Intelligent Career Card System (ICCS) help individuals and couples take ownership of these choices.

Understanding Career Choices with the Intelligent Career Card System (ICCS)

The Intelligent Career Card System (ICCS) helps individuals, and dual-career couples gain clarity on their career paths, what matters, and how to take ownership of their careers. The beauty of this approach is its flexibility: whether with an individual or a dual-career couple, it provides a structured and reflective way to break down career decisions.

As Michael Arthur, creator of the ICCS and author of *An Intelligent Career: Taking Ownership of Your Work and Your Life*, wrote, "A path with a heart is yours for the taking." This sentiment matched with Vanna's career dilemma.

The ICCS process posits three fundamental questions:

- Why do you work? (Understanding one's values, purpose, and motivation)
- How do you work? (Identifying skills, strengths and ways of learning)
- With whom do you work? (Assessing networks, collaborations, and career relationships)

Through a series of forced choice questions, individuals and couples sort and prioritize career themes to uncover themes and clarify choices. Unlike traditional career assessments, the ICCS provides a way to reflect on career motivators while also assessing choices within the organizational realities.

An Illustration of How This Might Work

Through coaching, I've seen how career clarity can transform a relocation decision. I recently worked with a couple where the woman, Vanna, was offered a role in Switzerland, while her partner had a promising position in New York. She was considering the move, and her partner encouraged her, thinking he could transfer to his firm's European office.

Vanna had spent over 15 years with a multinational food and beverage company, working in different countries. She had taken her current assignment in New York for its projects in Asia Pacific, but circumstances had changed. The firm was reducing its real estate portfolio and moving functions to Switzerland for tax benefits. Many of her colleagues were relocating, but she wasn't sure if she wanted to follow.

Vanna had been promoted every 2 years since joining and liked the company. But she now wanted a different role that played more to her analytical strengths (these aspirations typically surface in career conversations).

During our coaching sessions, Vanna mentioned that the Chief Operating Officer had stepped back from his role and asked her to take on more responsibilities. She welcomed it at first but soon found herself working alone in the New York office, managing remote teams across Asia and Latin America. The pressure increased, late nights and weekends. Short holidays or any family weekend hikes or getaways were put on hold. The move to Switzerland started to feel more like an escape than an opportunity.

When we spoke, she sounded excited. "I took over the COO's projects, and it's been non-stop travel and project management. I really enjoy it, but the teams haven't delivered on their side of the work." She sighed. "Yes, I'm frustrated, but looking forward to Switzerland." She paused and within the next breath said, "But I'm not sure about the move."

Her partner was willing to relocate. He'd said he was fine working remotely or that he'd find something new, also looking for what's next in his career. But she was worried. Was this the right move for him? Was it the right move for her?

Unpacking the Decision

Our meetings were on Zoom. As Vanna walked me through her career, a pattern emerged: big opportunities, bigger roles, constant promotions. But not once had she paused to ask herself what she wanted from her career.

"What makes you stay at the firm?" I asked.

She listed the projects, the travel, the people, the excitement of creating something new.

"Why did you join in the first place?"

She hesitated. "You know, I'm not sure. It was the offer. It was more money than I'd ever made, and I just kept moving up."

I let the moment settle.

"And before that? When you were in college, what did you want to do?"

She answered quickly almost without thinking,

"A doctor. I've always loved research and medicine."

I could hear the shift, a realization settling in. I'd say the penny dropped, but it was bigger than that. It was the first time she'd given herself permission to think. I suggested we use the Intelligent Career Card System to help clarify her motivations and uncover what mattered most in this next role.

For dual-career couples, the ICCS is a shared language and framework to examine career trade-offs and mobility decisions together. It is framed to help both partners manage career transitions which supports their shared ambitions rather than making them sacrifice one for the other.

Using the ICCS as part of the coaching process, Vanna and her partner made more informed decisions on next steps. While her partner supported the move, we focused on Vanna's next role. The following story illustrates how dual-career coaching can support couples in making career decisions together. Based on real coaching experiences, these narrative highlights common challenges and strategies, drawn from one partner's perspective.

	Vanna's top 3	*Partner's top 3*
Why do you work?	1. I want to be challenged in my work 2. I like to be involved in new business opportunity	1. I want to guarantee financial security 2. I want to make as much money as I can

(continued)

(continued)

	Vanna's top 3	Partner's top 3
How do you work?	3. I enjoy working in a supportive environment	3. I enjoy helping other people
	1. I seek to integrate information from different sources	1. I seek to improve my range of business skills
	2. I seek to become a more strategic thinker	2. I seek to become a better leader
	3. I seek to learn from people I work with	3. I seek to become a more strategic thinker
With Whom do you Work?	1. I give support to people I can help	1. I work to sustain my relationships with schools or college friends
	2. I work with people for whom I can learn	2. I build relationships with people more experienced than me
	3. I work with people to help solve their problems	3. I give support to people I can help

There are more points to consider under each segment, but I've only highlighted the top three points to demonstrate how this shaped Vanna's thinking on the potential role in Switzerland.

Career Insights Report: Vanna and Partner

What Drives Their Careers?

Vanna thrives in roles that stretch her strategic thinking and problem-solving skills, particularly in product expansion and innovation. While financial stability matters, she prioritizes growth and learning over security.

Her partner, in contrast, is financially driven, focusing on security, wealth-building, and leadership development. While both are committed to professional success, their motivations differ: Vanna seeks challenge and collaboration, while her partner prioritizes stability and advancement.

How Do They Work Best?

Vanna is a problem solver, constantly refining her communication and expertise. She enjoys decision-making roles that allow her to shape strategy, integrate diverse perspectives, and learn from others in a supportive environment.

Her partner takes a structured, skill-focused approach, aiming to broaden business acumen and leadership capabilities. His emphasis is on self-development and career progression within a clear framework.

Who Do They Work Best With?

Vanna is a natural mentor, excelling in collaborative environments where she can support, learn from, and develop others. Her leadership style is people-centric, emphasizing teamwork and alignment.

Her partner values relationship-building, particularly with more experienced professionals who support his leadership growth. While Vanna focuses on team cohesion, he leans towards networking for career progression.

Career Alignment and Coaching Insights

The coaching session was more focused on Vanna's career than her partner. He was happy with the prospect of moving to Switzerland, was currently working for an international firm and knew he could relocate there with little problem. Despite having differing drivers, both were highly adaptable and open to international mobility, an important ingredient for their career planning.

After the coaching engagement, I used ChatGPT to summarize insights from the ICCS data creating a summary of Vanna's career preferences. While her partner's employer provided a clear international path, Vanna faced greater complexity in assessing the potential move to Switzerland.

Ultimately, Vanna's firm underwent a restructuring, and her role was made redundant. They chose to remain in New York, where she found another role at a MNC with the potential for future international relocation. Her partner, meanwhile, stayed in his current role, continuing with his current employer.

The Intelligent Career Card Service Tool provided a structured framework asking questions on the why, how, and whom of both careers. This approach helped Vanna articulate her career goals and also identify areas of alignment and points of divergence with her partner. The coaching conversations uncovered their shared goals for a global career but also differences in how they defined success.

Dual-career coaching sessions are not always smooth sailing, often requiring an experienced executive coach and at times someone with a background in marriage and family counseling. Michael Arthur and Polly Parker's research into dual careers highlights the fine line coaches and counselors balance when working with dual-career couples. In their research, they recount a story about a dual-career couple, Jenny and Darren, whose career paths and expectations were not necessarily aligned.

In their article *Giving Voice to the Dual-Career Couple* Arthur and Parker's (2004) dual-career coaching research revealed differences in motivation, career priorities, and relationship expectations. Jenny and Darren valued working in an industry that mattered to them, but their definitions diverged. Jenny sought community respect and professional excitement whereas Darren prioritized stability and societal contribution.

- **Knowing-Why:** Both valued meaningful work but Jenny sought more career excitement and recognition, while Darren focused on providing for his family.
- **Knowing-How:** Darren felt stuck in his career, unsure of his next steps, while Jenny thrived in leadership. Through career exploration exercises, Darren identified new career paths, secured a new role, but it wasn't a perfect fit. Jenny realized she needed to develop broader leadership skills but struggled to define long-term goals.
- **Knowing-Whom:** Their discussion on networks and relationships revealed an imbalance. Jenny's professional connections supported her career while Darren had fewer external ties. Through the coaching, it became clear that something wasn't working in how they supported each other's professional growth, prompting a shift in their understanding of shared goals.

This case illustrates how career coaching for dual-career couples is rarely linear. Unlike individual coaching, it requires balancing two independent career paths while ensuring both partners remain aligned and supportive. As job markets fluctuate and career transitions arise, the ability to adapt together becomes essential.

As Parker and Arthur highlight, the psychological readiness of each partner varies as they interpret their responses across three segments. The goal is not to choose between career and marriage but to find fulfillment in both, a balance that at times may feel like walking a tightrope. This makes adaptive coaching coupled with a high degree of empathy, essential.

It is a given that a coach must listen attentively to both partners while also asking the right questions, two fundamental coaching skills. Asking thought-provoking questions and adapting to the nuances of both parties in each coaching session are also critical competencies for understanding the complexities of dual-career challenges. Empathy plays a central role, not only in coaching but also as a key competency of marriage and family therapists.

Additionally, effective coaches should bring a positive outlook, adaptability, organizational awareness, and conflict management skills, competencies identified in In Boyatzis et al.'s (2024) study, *Competencies of Coaches that Predict Client Behavior Change*. While not specific to dual-career coaching, these qualities are essential for coaches working with dual-career couples, as they help unpack individual and shared career goals, supporting alignment where needed and creating a space for meaningful dialogue. Organizations hiring a coach for dual-career engagements should prioritize these competencies to drive meaningful and effective coaching outcomes.

Reshaping Dual Career Support: From Policy to Coaching

In their article, *Making the Workplace Work for Dual-Career Couples*, Allocco et al. (2018), writing as part of Boston Consulting Group's research, outlined four priorities for change to meet the needs of this dynamic pool of talent. Similar to the Inclusive Leadership Compass framework, BCG took a broader view of workplace flexibility, organizational culture, and career development.

While the organisational element is important, I'm highlighting the need for a structured career decision-making tool to help dual career couples with transitions and choices to match their personal and professional needs. This shows a way for companies to create inclusive career paths and retain talent.

BCG has identified four change priorities for supporting dual-career couples:

1. **Change the Support: Leveraging Technology for Flexibility:** the value of technology-driven flexibility to enable dual-career success. Many organizations I've worked with embraced remote and hybrid work models, especially after the pandemic, making it easier for dual-career couples to balance work and personal commitments.
2. **Change How People Work: Rethinking Work Arrangements:** BCG's research underscores the importance of flexible schedules and nonlinear career models. Companies have incorporated these shifts, but some, particularly financial institutions, are rolling back flexibility and requiring a return to the office, reversing earlier progress. This highlights the ongoing tension between traditional work models and evolving employee needs.
3. **Change the Culture: Rewarding Outcomes Over Face Time:** BCG rightly emphasizes that lasting cultural change requires a refocus from face time to simply measuring results.
4. **Change What a Successful Career Path Looks Like:** The research calls for rethinking career progression, similar to the academic institutions that allow professors to pause tenure clocks without career penalties. Some professional service firms have enabled part-time work and career breaks without derailing long-term career paths and partnership potential. However, some organizations still view nontraditional career journeys with skepticism, questioning career gaps, time off for personal reasons, or alternative work trajectories.

This final point is where I see the biggest gap and the most significant opportunity. BCG's solid four-step framework helps companies structure dual-career practices within an organizational context. I'd recommend adding a structured coaching process for dual-career couples, enabling them to make informed choices on career transitions. Career decisions, whether taking time off, reducing hours, or transitioning roles, are not binary choices. By combining BCG's macro-level framework with career coaching, organizations can create inclusive, sustainable solutions that benefit both employees and the business.

THE FUTURE OF INCLUSION: RETHINKING TALENT MANAGEMENT FOR DUAL-CAREER GROWTH

Through the experiences of Min Seo, Vanna and the Parker & Arthur research, dual careers are no longer an exception but rather a growing global trend which organizations must address. Recognizing the value of dual-career couples and mid-career professionals requires rethinking traditional talent management practices. Flexible work arrangements remain important, but companies need to go further, embracing a more holistic and inclusive approach that acknowledges the interdependence of career decisions within households.

A global trend has emerged: talented women (and men) making career decisions not in isolation but as part of an 'organic unit, a two-person career reality'. Organizations that wish to recruit and retain top talent must adapt by introducing spousal hiring programs, flexible work options, relocation assistance for partners, and broader cultural support.

The evidence is clear: when companies address dual-career realities, they gain a competitive edge in attracting diverse talent and building loyalty. Conversely, those that ignore these realities risk losing high performers who seek opportunities that accommodate their whole family's needs. The message from research and case studies demonstrates that to hire one, you often must consider two.

The dynamics of dual-career couples are evolving, with both men and women increasingly considering their partner's career prospects before accepting new roles. While more women are declining opportunities when their partner's career is left out of the discussion, younger men are also making similar decisions, prioritizing dual-career balance. Same-sex partners face additional challenges, particularly in countries where legal recognition and visa access are restricted. In Hong Kong, a 2018 court ruling granted same-sex partners access to dependent visas, easing relocation. In contrast, the Philippines, the UAE, and 38 other countries across Asia do not legally recognize same-sex partnerships, making dual-career mobility even more challenging.

Final Thought: Academia as a Model for the Private Sector

Academic institutions have navigated dual-career hiring for decades and offer a compelling model for private-sector companies. As more women and younger employees demand dual-career accommodations, businesses may begin formalizing spousal hiring practices similar to those in academia. Many universities have established structured programs to support dual-career couples, recognizing that career mobility is a key factor in retaining academic excellence.

This institutional approach offers valuable lessons for companies seeking to attract and retain top talent in an increasingly mobile workforce. One example is the Higher Education Recruitment Consortium (HERC), a non-profit network of over 550 colleges and universities. HERC facilitates dual-career searches through job databases, networking opportunities, and career counseling services, enabling couples to secure employment within the same geographic region. Companies can learn from these practices, adapting them to corporate environments to create more inclusive and forward-thinking workplaces.

Implementing Dual-Career Coaching Support in Organizations

To translate these insights into action, organizations should consider the following:

- **Establish Dual-Career Coaching Team**: Develop a coaching-led resource hub to assist employees' partners with their career navigation, exploration and networking, ensuring access to personalized support.
- **Engage Experienced Career Coaches**: Partner with coaches experienced in working with dual-career couples, professionals who demonstrate the coaching competencies outlined by Boyatzis et al. (2024), such as empathy, adaptability, and a positive mindset.
- **Leverage Internal Networks & Industry Partnerships**: Create cross-company collaborations that provide career opportunities for employees' partners across sectors.

- **Promote Coaching Conversations on Dual Careers**: Encourage leaders and HR teams to discuss dual-career needs during recruitment and career conversations.

Inclusion means taking an expansive view of careers and understanding the shifts in the marketplace. Companies that integrate dual careers into their systems will not only attract and retain talented professionals but also shape a more forward-thinking, inclusive work environment. As Amartya Sen reminds us, *"The freedom to shape our lives is the most precious freedom we have."* This freedom extends to how individuals and organizations approach careers today. Supporting dual-career couples is not just a benefit; it is an inclusive practice that honors the evolving ways people build their futures together.

In the next chapter, we'll discuss an organizational culture change project with manufacturing leaders in the Philippines. Using the Inclusive Leadership Compass 360 Assessment, this case study demonstrates how inclusive practices can reshape behaviors and drive measurable cultural change.

References

Allocco, B., Lovich, D., Russell, M. S., & Brooks Taplett, F. (2018). *Making the workplace work for dual-career couples*. Boston Consulting Group.

Arthur & Parker: Parker, P., & Arthur, M. B. (2004). *Giving voice to the dual-career couple*. British Journal of Guidance & Counselling, 32(1), 3–23. https://doi.org/10.1080/03069880310001648102

Boyatzis, R. E., Liu, H., Smith, A., Zwygart, K., & Quinn, J. (2024). *Competencies of coaches that predict client behavior change*. The Journal of Applied Behavioral Science, 60(1), 19–49. evidencebasedmentoring.org+1peopledevelopmentinstitute.org+1

MOFA: Ministry of Foreign Affairs of Japan. (2022). *Support for dual-career families*. https://www.mofa.go.jp/

Schiebinger, L., Henderson, A. D., & Gilmartin, S. K. (2008). *Dual-career academic couples: What universities need to know*. Stanford University, Michelle R. Clayman Institute for Gender Research. https://gender.stanford.edu/sites/gender/files/dualcareerfinal_0.pdf

Sotirin, P., & Goltz, S. M. (2019). Academic dual career as a lifeworld orientation: A phenomenological inquiry. *The Review of Higher Education, 42*(3), 1207–1232. https://doi.org/10.1353/rhe.2019.0034

PART IV

Driving Cultural Change

CHAPTER 9

Building Sustainable Inclusion Through Culture Change

Change is disturbing when it is done to us, exhilarating when it is done by us.
Rosabeth Moss Kanter

How to Build Inclusion into the DNA of the Organization

Let's step away from theory and data for a moment and enter directly into a story. As highlighted in Chapter 2, sometimes the clearest lessons in inclusion emerge not from research, but from lived experience.

Reginald sat at the head of the table, arms crossed, as his managers rattled off production numbers, targets hit, machines running efficiently, error rates. The focus was purely on operations. But when someone mentioned employee concerns, long hours, lack of input, the mood shifted.

"Oh, come on, this again?" one manager said, exasperated. Another added, "We've heard it before. We can't change production schedules. If they don't like it, then…" His voice trailed off, and the room fell silent. Not in agreement, just uncertainty.

They knew something wasn't working. Turnover was high. Younger workers, uninterested in factory jobs, were leaving for tech roles or opportunities abroad. Those who stayed were disengaged, reluctant to speak up.

Reginald had spent his entire career in manufacturing, rising through the ranks in a command-and-control leadership style. But now, for the first time, he saw the cracks in the system.

He wasn't alone. Across the leadership team, there was a growing sense that what had worked before was no longer working. Retention was a symptom of something bigger, a leadership culture out of step with the workforce it needed to attract.

That's why I was brought in. Over the next 2 years, I worked with Reginald, his team, and 11 other factory leaders to rethink leadership and how they could create a workplace where people actually wanted to stay.

The Cultural Shift Begins

If inclusion was going to become embedded in the factory's DNA, it couldn't just be a policy change or a corporate initiative. It had to start with leaders themselves.

We began by examining leadership at the most fundamental level, self-awareness. Using the ILC 360, each leader had the opportunity to see their leadership through the eyes of their teams and uncover the behaviors that were either nurturing inclusion or pushing people away.

We kicked off the session with three guiding questions:

- As leaders, what do we stand for?
- What changes do we need—not just want—to make in our factories, and why?
- How will we turn these ideas into action?

All straightforward and almost predictable consulting questions, but not easy to answer. Addressing them laid the foundation for a shift that would impact not just the leaders in the room, but the entire factory culture. Fortunately, the ILC 360 help to identify behaviors and pinpoint areas for change both individually and organizationally. We used the assessment over a 2-year period to measure results.

Setting the Stage: The ILC 360 Assessment
The project began with 15 leaders across factories in the Philippines, each had received feedback from 10 to 18 respondents. For many of these leaders, it was their first experience with a 360° feedback process,

along with getting their heads around inclusive leadership. Despite the hierarchical culture in the Philippines, where staff is often reluctant to speak candidly about their leaders, the feedback was remarkably candid and insightful, shedding light on developmental opportunities for the leadership. The ILC framework provided a solid platform across four dimensions of leadership: self, others, team, and organization.

Reading through the verbatim comments, the patterns of command-and-control were obvious, an overly rigid process and low tolerance for mistakes which is necessary for operations but a disincentive to achieve any meaningful innovation or collaboration. New employees had ideas to improve efficiency, but usually remained quiet, fearing push back from management.

Reading through the verbatim comments, patterns of command-and-control leadership with an overly rigid process and low tolerance for mistakes. While this may serve operational needs, it acts as a disincentive for collaboration. Several new employees mentioned having ideas to but chose to remain quiet, fearing pushback from management. A few mentioned in the feedback, "he needs to create a space where different opinions can be expressed, heard and valued. 'He needs to intentionally seek out perspectives from those who are different from him."

The factory leaders typically dominated discussions, mistakes were publicly dissected, and new ideas were dismissed with "It's been done before" or "not time for experimentation; it would be nice, but we don't have the luxury of time." This baseline assessment offered a clear starting point for the changes needed.

The biggest issue was high turnover and an inability to attract employees. But this wasn't just about retention and hiring, it was about a leadership culture that was out of step. Aspiring professionals in the Philippines preferred careers in tech or sought opportunities abroad, rather than joining a factory that felt rigid, transactional, and outdated. This wasn't just a local problem. A Deloitte study found that 80% of respondents consider inclusion important when choosing an employer, and 39% would leave their current organization for a more inclusive one. More than half of those surveyed said they would leave their job for a workplace with a stronger culture of inclusion (Deloitte 2018).

The leadership approach created a workplace where employees had little autonomy, and the focus was solely on production. Most managers saw their work as simply 'making biscuits' reinforcing a mindset where people were secondary to processes.

The CEO was acutely aware that few people wanted to work in their factories, and even fewer wanted to stay in an environment that didn't respect their contributions. In an area with plenty of other manufacturing options, employees had the freedom to leave, and they did. Attracting and retaining talent required more than just policy changes or better compensation; it demanded a radical cultural shift toward a workplace where employees felt valued, heard, and invested in.

To start the process of making the factories a better place to work, I encouraged the leadership to answer a fundamental question: "*What do we stand for?*"

Methodology: Creating Impetus for Change

We rolled out the ILC 360 under tight timelines, and to our surprise, all responses were submitted by the deadline, rarely seen with other firms. To me, that one factor showed an unusual commitment to their change initiative.

We typically give individual coaching sessions and debrief leaders on their results, but this group preferred a group debrief. I wasn't sure if that was a good idea, as leaders I've worked with wouldn't want to receive feedback about inclusivity in a public setting and this particular leadership had never even been through a 360 process.

I agreed with their request, but with a twist: we organized smaller cohorts, creating peer learning circles that turned out to be the best way to have delivered the feedback. These groups became both sparring partners and learning partners, which sparked the change process.

Our first session set the context. We grouped the leaders into quartets to review their assessments and began each meeting adhering to Kline's method using a quick round of positive questions *"What would make this session worthwhile?"* or '*What might keep you from being present in this meeting?*" Once everyone one responded (without interruptions) we started the debriefing process.

Throughout the 2 years of working with this leadership group, meetings or one to one conversation began with positive rounds and uninterrupted listening. This approach modeled the inclusive processes we wanted them to adopt with their own teams. We used Kline's methods of paired discussions, dialogue sessions, and a Thinking Council, reinforcing the importance of listening and asking thoughtful questions to build inclusion with their teams. After months of applying this, they saw how this foundation of trust allowed diverse ideas to bubble up.

Before we began the first debrief, we asked 'how would you define inclusion? and 'how would you define exclusion?' The responses about inclusion were similar to what we'd previously heard: *"being part,"* *"involved,"* *"I belong,"* or in Tagalog, *"kabarkada",* which refers to a close friend or someone in your social circle, symbolizing belonging. The group chose this word as a starting point for building an inclusive factory. Some even suggested using it on a t-shirt. In his book *The Trusted Advisor*, David Maister explains that when envisioning a new reality, (as this group was doing) use a slogan or a sound bite to show the value of the change in a visible way. Their t-shirt idea made perfect sense.

Their discussion on exclusion was much more emotional. Words like "sad," "disengaged," or "hayaan" (Tagalog for "let them be") stood out. Participants explained that *hayaan* was often meant with good intentions, a way of respecting someone's space, avoiding interference, or allowing them to figure things out on their own.

One participant reflected, "You need to understand, 'let them be' is like tossing them aside and hoping they make it. I realize now how 'letting them be' might actually be the reason why people shut down. In this culture, people won't speak up when they feel excluded, they stay silent, stop trying, and eventually leave." As the conversation continued, the team collectively recognized their assumptions—believing that employees from different provinces wouldn't understand factory life. 'We thought we were respecting their space by not interfering,' one participant said, 'but now I see that by simply *letting them be*, we were making them feel like outsiders before they even had a chance to belong.'

The change conversation started here. This was a tight-knit group of factory management with many living nearby. In many ways, this was their community, their family. But they soon saw how their close-knit ways shut others out. These conversations became a turning point. The words *kabarkada* and *hayaan* became touchstones we revisited throughout the year to keep their changes on track.

Reginald's Story: How One Leadership Team's Shift Unlocked Cultural Change

Before he took the assessment, we had several conversations to help Reginald and his team feel comfortable with the process. As I worked more with the team, I could see they were clear about their goal: to create a culture that attracts and retains younger talent. The simple act of writing down a goal made a difference. Reinforcing their commitment and clarifying their focus. They also understood the need to move from a top-down, transactional leadership approach to a bottom-up inclusive approach. Transactional leaders tend to focus on rewards tied to specific outcomes, closely monitoring performance and stepping in to solve problems. While this approach has its merits, it rarely prioritizes inclusivity. Since inclusion was identified as a strategic driver to address low engagement scores and high attrition rates, Reginald (and others) recognized the need for change. This wasn't just a hunch; it was backed by data.

Reginald was in charge of three factories out of 19 production sites and part of the manufacturing and supply chain leadership team. At the start of our engagement, he told me he had no idea what it meant to be inclusive or why the company had even bothered to do any of this. Reginald was skeptical. *"I don't get it,"* he told me after our first session. *"Inclusion? We run factories, we hit targets and get the job done." Everyone is included to make this happen."* He wasn't resistant to change, but he didn't see the point. It took a long time for Reginald to unpack the concept of inclusion.

But in one of our early sessions, something shifted. One of the team members, a rising leader in the factory, spoke up for the first time: *"Sir, some of my team members have ideas, but no one speaks up and if they do, they worry that it's seen as complaining."*

The group went silent. This wasn't an outsider pushing an idea, this was one of their own, voicing something many felt. Reginald listened. That was the first step in the change process. He started listening more and observed how the team interacted. He also realized silence wasn't compliance but disengagement.

Reginald's career began in a manufacturing site in Negros Occidental, a 90-minutes flight from Manila. Over the years, he worked in Dubai and Europe before returning to the Philippines to oversee three manufacturing sites at the food manufacturing firm. Known for his humor and quick temper, Reginald had coaching before and was open to feedback.

His energy and stamina were legendary, known for being 'always on', never taking a day off and expecting the same from others. If Reginald was at the factory at 6 AM, his team followed suit. The schedule and the lack of work-life balance became a running joke. When I mentioned work-life balance to the team, they rolled their eyes and laughed. Reginald smirked and said, "Work-life what? Is that a new production metric?" while someone else chimed in, "Sure, we'll schedule 'balance' right after the next 12-hour shift!"

When Reginald received his 360 feedback, he was pleasantly surprised. Some team members rated him as inclusive and supportive, while others, including his boss, did not. His self-assessment reflected this contrast; he rated himself lower on Self-Awareness, which aligned with his own reflections. The verbatim comments and scores gave him a clear picture of both his strengths and development areas.

Technically skilled but disconnected from others' views, Reginald had spent decades in manufacturing and supply chain management, refining his ability to solve technical problems and drive efficiency. But he also believed that a big part of leadership was being the smartest person on the factory floor. He rarely acknowledged mistakes, and the feedback reflected that:

- *He's technically competent but doesn't interact much with people who are different from him.*
- *His hands are full juggling many roles, he tries to do everything himself, and that's just not sustainable.*

Reginald's leadership style created a culture where employees waited for his direction. His "always-on" energy, though impressive, often silenced others, inadvertently making it difficult for his team to step up, contribute, and develop. This was also reflected in the feedback:

Highly skilled and deeply committed, he is an energetic leader who makes decisive calls when challenges arise.

But while Reginald's team largely saw him as an effective leader with a few areas for growth, his boss was more critical, believing he fell short of expectations.

Who was his boss? The Head of Manufacturing and Supply Chain, who had a traditional view of leadership. He thought Reginald should be directive and execution focused but not mired in daily operations.

The disconnect between the boss's view and the team's perspective reminded me of other organizations I worked with in the Asia Pacific Region. Despite being respected and admired by their teams. Was Reginald being held to an unreasonably high standard, or was his boss assessing leadership through a narrow lens, one that overlook inclusivity, trust, and, ultimately, humanity? This pattern isn't uncommon. In Chapter 5, Aileen's boss's boss had a narrow definition of leadership, overlooking her strengths in favor of more 'traditional' attributes. While Reginald's situation was different, the core question remained: Was his boss evaluating him through a biased framework that prioritized authority? Or was he genuinely setting the bar high for Reginald's development as a leader?

In Reginald's case, I'd say yes and no. The issue wasn't that his boss set an unfairly high bar, rather that Reginald too steeped in the details. Continuing this pattern would ultimately limit both his and the team's development.

Transition into the Peer Learning Sessions

Once we started a series of peer learning sessions, we structured three facilitated sessions over nine months, with each session focusing on a specific action item.

We began with Reginald and his core team, Charles, Henry, and Joyce, by conducting a group debrief on their strengths.

- **Joyce** was viewed as the empathic one, the 'glue' who held both the team and the factory together.
- **Charles** was thought to be humble and an introspective thinker.
- **Henry** was recognized as an adaptable problem-solver with a growth mindset.

Starting with strengths allowed the team to see and appreciate each other's unique contributions. The peer group debrief played a role in this process, giving them the opportunity to recognize each other's strengths in a way that wouldn't have been possible through individual coaching sessions. They relied on Joyce's empathic insights to better understand the needs of factory employees, drew on Charles' ability to step back and analyze situations with a critical eye, and leaned on Henry's adaptability to navigate challenges in real time. By harnessing these strengths, they began working together in new ways, reinforcing a connected leadership team with a shared focus on shaping a new factory culture.

For most, this realization seemed obvious, but for Reginald, it was a revelation. Having spent years calling the shots, he believed leadership was about driving results and making decisions. The idea that a connected leadership team, built on shared strengths and responsibilities, was just as critical as execution marked a major shift in his thinking.

After identifying the team's strengths, we moved to developmental opportunities. Reginald's leadership style set the tone for the team, and his tendency to dominate discussions influenced others, including Henry. While Reginald was the primary driver of this dynamic, Henry also struggled to integrate diverse perspectives and manage dominant voices in meetings.

At the same time, the team's feedback highlighted areas for growth. Reginald and Joyce were rated high in self-awareness but lower on respect and giving others autonomy. Charles and Henry scored lower on self-awareness, respect, and personalization. Charles was perceived as 'distant' and overly focused on finances, while Henry's difficulty in managing different perspectives reinforced the team's existing dynamic. Though Reginald's influence was strong, Henry's own approach contributed to limiting open discussions.

Like Reginald, Joyce had worked in the factory a long time and was thus an 'on-the-floor' problem solver, but their staff wanted to tackle problems themselves and have more access to career development opportunities. Not just 'training' but access to networking opportunities with other leaders and participate in high profile projects.

Reginald's team focused on the mistakes themselves rather than coaching others to learn from their mistakes. This became a focal point for the group, which is fundamental in an environment where an incremental mistake is extremely costly for both business and employees.

Self-Awareness in the ILC is defined as having a strong awareness of oneself and impact on others. As we looked into the group's development areas, we saw a consistent thread that needed to be addressed: respect and personalization to engage others and recognize their potential.

Looking at the collective feedback from Reginald's team, employees emphasized the need for greater autonomy and inclusion in decision-making. While Joyce had started to step back, the broader concern was that decision-making remained concentrated at the top. The team wanted more opportunities to contribute, rather than simply execute directives. Additionally, the responses demonstrated a genuine concern for their leaders' well-being and balance. The leaders were seen as 'always-on,' leaving little time to connect with their teams. Employees worried that this constant state of busyness was unsustainable and would ultimately impact both effectiveness and the factory's success.

In the peer learning sessions, we spent time on an 'appreciative management approach' to problem solving, one that focuses on understanding the individual's needs rather than jumping to an immediate fix. Depending on the scale of the issue, this can be a balancing act. At first, the approach was met with resistance; some felt it was 'too kind and too slow.' Ultimately, though, it was their commitment to action that made a difference.

For Reginald, Charles, Henry, and Joyce, this meeting was not simply to discuss behaviors but choose actions they'd agreed to implement. To reinforce accountability, the team identified obstacles and workarounds. One question that played out through the entire change journey was *"As a leadership team, what do we stand for?"* which led to some reflection of *"What are the roadblocks that could get in our way of achieving this?"*

They chose one initiative and made a date to review the impact. Subsequent sessions followed the same format, identifying a development opportunity and structuring their approach around four questions:

1. **Who's** involved?
2. **What's** the specific action?
3. **When** do we check in with one another?
4. **How** will we measure our impact?

As they worked through their plans, the team began framing questions around inclusion, such as:

- *What does an inclusive meeting look like?*
- *If we approached problems inclusively, how would our solutions be different?*

By the end of the peer learning sessions, their leadership evolution was no longer just about learning new behaviours it was about transforming how they led, engaged, and included others.

By Year 2, there were noticeable improvements. Reginald and his team moved from a directive, top-down leadership style to a more facilitative one. Their teams now described them as more open and a few even mentioned inclusive.

How the Team Shifted

- **Charles,** previously viewed as distant and hesitant to engage in peer coaching, altered his approach. One respondent noted: "Charles now asks for our input rather than assuming he has all the answers. We've seen a change in how he leads."
- **Henry** received feedback on his progress: "He's more willing to listen, open to suggestions, and allows the team to grow."
- **Joyce,** once the empathic glue holding the team together, learned to step back and trust the team's strengths. By giving them more autonomy, she allowed the team to make decisions while holding back from criticizing mistakes.
- **Reginald,** whose leadership was once described as overly directive and 'always on,' had perhaps the most dramatic shift. In the past, he made all the decisions himself, expected immediate compliance, and rarely sought input. Two years later, the feedback reflected a different leader:

> *When an important situation in the plant arises, whether for improvement or problem resolution, he brings clarity in roles and offers support to his team. He's an observant leader with a keen ability to assess situations and respond quickly.*

This feedback was significant. Instead of controlling every decision, Reginald had learned to step back and guide rather than dictate. His shift from command-and-control to facilitative leadership was a major change, one that didn't happen overnight but was reinforced through peer learning, and real-time application of inclusive leadership practices.

As the sessions progressed the team realized, while individual leadership development was essential, the real opportunities (and challenges) lay within the culture itself.

All 15 leaders across the factories could define who they wanted to be as leaders but kept returning to one critical question: *What might get in our way of achieving this change?*

McKinsey data shows that 70% of organizational change initiatives fail to achieve their objectives, making this question even more relevant. While high failure rates are often attributed to employee resistance and management behaviors, in this case the leaders' response was clear: *"This is the way we work around here."*

That simple reflection marked a turning point. The conversation shifted from individual leadership behaviors to shared norms that shape how work gets done. It was no longer just about personal development, but about challenging the cultural assumptions embedded in daily routines. We framed the discussion using Edgar Schein's change model, focusing on the underlying assumptions and unspoken rules that reinforced those behaviors.

There were three underlying assumptions reinforcing the status quo:

1. **Work Hours:** Believing long hours signaled dedication, rather than inefficiency and poor well-being.
2. **Mistakes:** Framing mistakes as failures rather than learning and growth opportunities.
3. **Hierarchy:** A culture that limited input to senior leaders instead of all levels of the organization.

Strategy consultants and coaches emphasize the importance of addressing both the rational and emotional aspects of change, helping individuals and groups make sense of it all. One way to do this is to ask, '*Is there evidence to support the need for change?*'

In this case, a high turnover rate and low engagement at the factory was the evidence. To build the culture we introduced a structured approach, The Thinking Council, with the same group of 15 leaders allowed all of them a way to discuss potential barriers and uncover collective solutions.

The Thinking Council is similar to the Clearing Process or Action Learning Practice, in which a leader presents a challenge and receives input from diverse participants. One rule applies: participants may only ask questions, not offer advice or solutions. This in itself required a behavioral shift in how they approached problem-solving. Rather than assuming they have all the answers, they adopted an 'ask, not tell' approach, a departure from how this group of leaders typically behaved. This practice pushes leaders toward a coaching-oriented process that supports greater inclusion.

Facilitating a Thinking Council: A Structured Approach to Surface Insights
We split the 15 leaders into two structured groups to address assumptions that could hinder their change projects. One leader focused on working hours, another on minimizing mistakes, two critical issues they faced.

The Thinking Council helped tackle a third underlying assumption: hierarchy. Getting input from a diverse group of employees allowed colleagues from different backgrounds to share a range of perspectives. Unlike traditional problem solving where quick solutions are expected, the Thinking Council focused on slowing down the process by asking the right questions, engaging in generative listening, and resisting the urge to give immediate answers.

Why Questions Instead of Solutions?
I worked with each leader to frame the question, one that would push beyond surface-level solutions:

- **Working Hours:** *How can we move from a culture that equates long hours with loyalty to one that values efficiency and well-being?*
- **Mistakes:** *How can we create an environment where mistakes are seen as an opportunity to learn rather than a failure to be punished?*

At first, this approach felt unnatural, particularly with leaders who were used to making decisions and expecting answers. But by structuring the process in seven key steps, we helped them shift their mindset.

Step 1: Framing the Challenge: Each leader outlined the core challenge they faced. The rest of the group (the Council) listened to understand the context. The leader's role was to articulate why this issue mattered and what change they were seeking.
Step 2: Crafting the Right Question: I worked with each leader to frame a question that would guide the Council's thinking. The question needed to be open-ended and amenable to receiving insights rather than an immediate solution.

Step 3: Clarifying Understanding: The leader presented their respective question to the Council. Before diving into responses, we facilitated a round of clarifying questions to make certain everyone understood the challenge. As the facilitator, I checked with the leader to confirm whether the clarifications aligned with their intent. If needed, we could adjust the question to capture the challenge effectively.

Step 4: Silent Reflection: The Council took a few minutes to reflect on the question before jotting down their initial thoughts. This pause gave everyone more thinking time rather than forcing a hurried solution.

Step 5: The Thinking Rounds: Following the Thinking Environment principles, we conducted rounds where each Council member responded to the leader with a question, structured to provoke more thinking than solving. We used the "no-interruption rule."

Step 6: Checking for New Insights: Once complete, I asked the leader: "What are your thoughts on working hours or mistakes now?" allowing them to say if their perspective changed and whether new options were possible. Since we had additional time, I asked if the question was still relevant or if they needed further insights from the Council, which led to a second round to build on the ideas generated.

Step 7: Closing with Insights and Appreciation: At the close of the session, each Council member wrote down 1–3 takeaways for the leader, along with a note of appreciation, highlighting a quality they valued in both the leader and others in the Council. The reflections and appreciations were handed to the leader. Written notes of appreciation reinforced the practice of appreciative feedback.

What This Looked Like in Practice

During one session, a plant manager wrestled with his team's resistance to reporting mistakes. He had assumed they were simply careless until he started asking questions.

"I used to think my team just wasn't paying attention," he admitted. *"But when I finally asked them why mistakes weren't being reported, the answers were different than I expected."*

One worker told him: *"Sir, the last time someone reported a mistake, he got called out in front of the team. After that, no one wanted to be next."*

The manager sat with that for a moment before posing his own question to the Thinking Council:

> We've built our systems around catching and fixing errors, but have we also built a culture where reporting mistakes feels too risky? How do we create an environment where speaking up isn't seen as failure?

That small turn, asking a question that challenged his own assumptions, opened up new conversations. Instead of debating how to make reporting easier, the group focused on building greater trust and openness within their factory operations.

Shifting Leadership Mindsets

I've used the Thinking Council method with many groups facing complex challenges, a structured yet open process which allows leaders to break out of entrenched thinking and listen to new perspectives. The Council practice of asking questions, rather than jumping to solutions provides time to think, the essence of inclusion.

In *A Hidden Wholeness*, Parker Palmer describes the Clearness Committee, a practice rooted in the seventeenth century Quaker tradition. The goal is to ask honest, open-ended questions, not to offer solutions, guiding an individual toward clarity.

The Thinking Council shares this spirit of inquiry but is distinct in its structure and purpose. While Palmer's method is about personal discernment, the Thinking Council is designed for organizational leadership, tackling systemic challenges, and shifting group decision-making culture.

As Palmer writes: *"The soul speaks its truth only under quiet, inviting, and trustworthy conditions."* I found this to be true in our sessions. When leaders stopped speaking and started listening, the real issues surfaced.

When leaders are used to giving instructions or being the expert, stepping back can feel uncomfortable. Knowing how to ask the right questions takes time and discipline but when done correctly, it transforms how leaders think.

The answers already exist, the role of the Thinking Council is to let them rise to the surface. This does more than just provide an answer; it changes decision-making habits, and it challenges beliefs, disbeliefs, and biases, the things that often block progress. It sounds simple, but I guarantee you it's not easy to learn.

For this group of leaders, it also challenged their underlying assumptions about hierarchy. They had been conditioned to believe that decision-making should remain at the top, limiting input from those at other levels of the organization. The Thinking Council experience pushed them to see leadership as more participatory, reinforcing that solutions and insights could emerge from anywhere in the organization, not just senior leaders.

By shifting to reflective inquiry, leaders begin to build inclusion creating time for real dialogue that continued long after the session ended. This practice didn't just create better decisions it helped reshape their leadership mindset, making inclusion a lived experience rather than just something they talked about.

Measuring Impact: Year 2 Results

Many organizations I've worked with ask whether inclusion can be measured. The answer is a definitive yes. A structured approach, which I've already outlined, makes inclusion both observable and quantifiable.

Research shows that sustained behavioral change typically takes an average of 66 days, according to a study by Dr. Phillippa Lally and her team at University College London. Their research, published in the *European Journal of Social Psychology*, found that while the time frame varies depending on the complexity of the behavior, it takes approximately 2 months for a new habit to become automatic, with some behaviors requiring up to 254 days to take root. Thus the importance of peer-learning, long-term tracking and continuous feedback in achieving lasting change.

To make it measurable, we created a five-step measurement framework, combining multiple data sources to track behavioral shifts and organizational impact:

1. **Baseline Assessment**—First was the Inclusive Leadership Compass (ILC) assessment, capturing behaviors linked to inclusion and providing a data-driven starting point.
2. **Time-Based Tracking**—Given that change requires reinforcement over time, the peer learning partners will challenge old behaviours and guide progress.
3. **Multi-Method Measurement**:

- **Behavioral Assessments**, (ILC assessment), Pulse & Engagement Surveys tracked across each factory to gauge the impact of inclusion.
- **Observational Data**, teams observed leadership interactions at meetings and any visible shifts in decision-making practices
- **Qualitative Feedback**, employees shared experiences on how this shift in leadership style impacted them and the team.

4. **Impact Analysis**, comparing data across the assessments offered insights particularly in factory settings versus an executive team.
5. **Action & Reinforcement** these insights informed leadership development through individual and peer coaching and other programs to sustain change.

One year after the initial ILC assessment, we conducted a second round to measure progress. The results showed improvements across most dimensions, particularly in self-awareness and organizational impact. Leaders demonstrated greater openness, active listening and a willingness to share decision-making responsibilities. This structured, multi-method approach marked a measurable change in leadership and teams they managed. Inclusion wasn't abstraction. It was observable and quantifiable.

The only area where scores dipped slightly was under the team dimension of the ILC, a likely reflection of growing pains as teams adjusted to the new leadership approach.

When comparing the scores from 2023 to 2024, we observed a notable increase from 3.97 to 4.06, moving closer to the global average of 4.23 (ILC team data).

The aggregated reports showed that Self and Other scores improved, while Organization scores remained stable. One of the hardest behaviors to shift was the association between long work hours and loyalty. While leaders made progress, the expectation of employees to be on-call for operational breakdowns remained.

Refining Engagement Surveys for Inclusion

After the first year, I worked with another factory leader, Rodel, who was strongly committed to the inclusion changes. Following his debrief, he asked to discuss his factory's engagement survey and asked how we could refine it to better measure inclusion.

While we planned for a broader ILC impact assessment in Year 2, Rodel wanted to track early progress at his factory. I didn't think enough time had passed to measure the change but Rodel's instinct to change the survey questions made sense. After reviewing the survey, we suggested refining several items to explicitly incorporate inclusive behaviors. The table below outlines these refinements:

Original survey item	Refined for inclusion
Follows policies and procedures	Ensure policies and procedures are inclusive
Maintains self-control in conversations	All voices are heard with no interruptions
Engages in regular conversations with the team	Generate a constructive exchange of diverse views
Makes decisions that positively impact team performance	Make sure the team's perspectives are part of the decision-making
Encourages subordinates to obtain necessary skills and training	Provide teams with opportunities for development
Encourages others to share ideas for team cohesion	Create an environment where everyone feels comfortable speaking up, sharing ideas, and asking questions without any finger-pointing

At the end of Year 2, Rodel noted a slight increase in overall engagement. More importantly, turnover remained stable, which was one of the biggest concerns and impetus for the change initiative. Rodel mentioned they were not expecting an overnight transformation, but the small improvements showed they were moving in the right direction.

Conclusion: Progress, Not Perfection

This change project was unique not just because of the frameworks used but because of the time invested in the process. Unlike many organizations that rush to implement change, this firm allowed *2 years* for leaders to internalize new behaviors and drive cultural shifts.

While some challenges, like work-hour expectations were still present, leaders recognized that to alter a corporate culture, properly, takes time. The bottom line was that sustainable inclusion comes from ongoing commitment rather than immediate perfection.

Lessons Learned from Other Organizations

Across different contexts and industries, I've seen how leadership behaviors shape inclusion, even when culture change isn't the stated goal. In two separate engagements, a leadership feedback tool revealed how everyday actions can either support or get in the way of inclusion.

Reinforcing Strengths Through Humility

In one case, we worked with a group of senior leaders and their direct reports. Each leader received an individual coaching session, followed by small peer learning session turning insights into action. Like others we've worked with, these leaders chose two or three actions based on the feedback, then shared this commitment with their team and manager.

As we worked with this group of leaders, the data surfaced themes that might have otherwise gone unnoticed. Two consistent strengths emerged: humility and openness. While the organization wasn't focused on culture change, the insights provided a glimpse into a culture already on the path toward demonstrating inclusion.

Feedback Highlights

- "She always acknowledges the work of others and gives credit where it's due."
- "He listens more than he speaks and encourages open debate in a way that makes everyone feel valued."

Rather than focusing on behavioral gaps, they found ways to amplify strengths, applying the same humility in high-impact moments in talent reviews, performance evaluations, and cross-functional collaboration. In doing so, humility became both personal and structural, shaping how leaders sought input, made better decisions, and expanded opportunities for talent across the organization.

Bridging the Inclusion Perception Gap

With another client we used the same feedback process with a group of leaders who had not previously participated in structured leadership assessment. Most believe they were inclusive, but their teams experienced things differently. They believed they had created an open and safe environment where all voices were heard, but the feedback showed otherwise.

Feedback Highlights
- "Most on his team are not comfortable speaking up."
- "Decisions are made at the top."

This disconnect wasn't just about perception, it was about impact. Corroborating Zenger and Folkman research, these leaders saw themselves as inclusive, but their behaviors landed differently with their teams. A recurring pattern in the debrief sessions that they tended to dominate meetings and prioritize the loudest voices, ultimately shaping decision-making.

What We Learned from This Group

The debrief/coaching session provided opportunities for leaders to reflect. Over time, small but deliberate changes emerged. A few leaders I worked with applied Kline's approach, incorporating rounds and positive questions in meetings to engage quieter team members. They broadened decision-making beyond their immediate group and became more appreciative in their feedback approach.

Although this project did not explicitly target organizational culture change, these individual shifts reinforced what we already knew: it is behaviors, not policies, that create the conditions for inclusion.

THE BROADER LESSON: CULTURAL CHANGE IS LEADERSHIP IN ACTION

These experiences reinforce a universal truth about cultural change: it's not easy, but it's possible with intent, persistence, and the courage to stretch leadership muscles. Cultural change must begin with leadership, as they set the pace but it's the *how* of introducing change, as Rosabeth Moss Kanter emphasizes, that makes all the difference. When people feel that change is imposed upon them, resistance is inevitable. However, when people are invited to shape it, change becomes something they can welcome and sustain.

We've seen this clearly in organizations, and it holds true in broader societal contexts. Top-down mandates and strong-arming people, whether in business or government, rarely lead to lasting transformation. Real change happens when leaders include people as active participants and co-creators of the future. Whether in factories in the Philippines or within national governments, the most enduring transformations occur when people feel empowered, included, and invested.

Cultures, like policies, thrive not through imposition but through shared commitments. When leaders create the right conditions for change rather than forcing it, the results are not only sustainable but transformative. When leaders consciously and collaboratively shift the culture, they unlock new possibilities for inclusion, engagement, and stronger business outcomes from talent retention to innovation and long-term growth.

LOOKING AHEAD: INCLUSION, COACHING, AND AI IN THE C-SUITE

As organizations continue to adapt to workforce demographics, the role of AI in coaching and behavioral nudges for inclusive leaders is more relevant than ever. In the next chapter, we look at the C-suite perspective on inclusive leadership, the impact of coaching and AI, drawing from their experiences, research, and lessons learned. These combined perspectives provide a window on what's shaping the future of inclusive leadership and organizational culture.

REFERENCE

Deloitte. (2018). Inclusion Pulse Survey findings: importance of inclusion in attracting and retaining talent. Deloitte. https://www2.deloitte.com/insights (or the specific Deloitte URL where the survey data appears)

PART V

Technology and Leadership Insights

CHAPTER 10

Leaders' Perspectives on Inclusion, Coaching, and AI

The quality of results produced by any system depends on the quality of awareness from which people in the system operate.
Otto Scharmer

Fifty years ago, in his seminal work on *transformational leadership*, James MacGregor Burns wrote that "Leadership is one of the most observed and least understood phenomena on earth." Half a century later, this remains a truism in today's complex landscape. Defining leadership is never straightforward, as discussed in Chapter 6 with Aileen, where we touched upon the ambiguity of what it means to be a leader.

Burns described leadership as a symbiotic relationship, elevating the motivation and morality between leader and follower. This is, to me, the essence of inclusion. Inclusion can bring that all-important element of humanity back into the leadership equation, reinforcing Burns' definition by bridging strengths across teams and organizations. After all, leadership is, at its core, a unique moral connection between individuals and teams. Without such a sturdy connection, engagement suffers, and work relationships become hollow.

I have spent decades interviewing leaders throughout my career, seeking to understand the values and experiences which have shaped them. Three years ago, I shifted my focus to inclusive leadership, interviewing more than 30 leaders in business, academia, NGOs, religious communities and professional practices. My background is in the corporate sector, but I believe in the benefits of cross fertilization of ideas. I've found the most valuable insights emerge at the intersections of disciplines. My narrative approach is to ask open-ended questions and allow a story to unfold.

This chapter captures the essence of such stories to see what we can learn from their experiences. In addition to a structured interview, I used expert research on coaching impact on behavioral change, on leadership and the emerging role of AI in coaching and leadership development.

During these conversations, the one point made abundantly clear was that inclusion is not an idealistic concept. It is a leadership choice, influencing decision-making, team culture and organizational success. While some may find inclusion easier to incorporate, others learn to develop it over time. The following stories illustrate two realities: that exclusion fuels resilience and growth, and that inclusion (when applied intentionally) transforms leadership.

Hiding in Plain Sight: The Cost of Assimilation and How Exclusion Fuels Resilience

George, a UK national, is a polished and strategic leader. As a gay man, he learned early in his consulting career to navigate environments where authenticity came with risk. A senior partner once made it clear that bringing his full self to work wasn't an option. That experience shaped his approach to leadership. Now a decade later and leading an innovation lab in London, George brings a more open presence sharing his story, creating space for others to be heard and seen. Today, he's more comfortable sharing with others how to balance the realities of business with the need for belonging.

The Waiting Game: When Opportunities Comes from Elsewhere

John spent years climbing the corporate ladder at a global agriculture firm in North America. Despite his advanced degrees and solid results, he hit a plateau. As an African American man, he took pride in his company's public commitment to diversity but felt equally frustrated by being consistently placed in the "high potential with more room to grow" quadrant of the 9-box talent grid. After a mentor encouraged him to take a role in Singapore, John relocated to Singapore and thrived. The move gave him the opportunity he had been denied, proving that he was more than ready for a leadership role. From the agriculture firm, he went on to lead in several global firms.

Leading Across Borders: Inclusion as a Way of Working

Angelina, born and raised in Hong Kong, built a global career marked by adaptability, openness, and cultural fluency. From Hong Kong to Canada, the UK to Dubai, Singapore and back again, each transition shaped not just her experience but her leadership. Starting in consulting, she was promoted every few years. It wasn't just her technical skills, her ability to bring people together across cultures, roles, and teams became her defining strength. By the time she joined a global investment bank in Hong Kong, inclusion wasn't just a corporate value; it was how she led.

Each story captures a different dimension of inclusion in leadership, whether it's individual resilience, and cross-cultural adaptability, or the recognition of overlooked talent. These are not abstract examples; I interviewed and worked closely with each of these leaders, and in one case served as their coach during a pivotal career transition. Like other leaders, their experiences shaped who they are today, and for each one, it was coaching or mentoring that offered a sounding board for growth.

The above stories match the experiences leaders I interviewed for this book. Each worked with a coach at some point in their career, particularly during leadership transitions. Most sought coaching support when moving from an individual contributor role to leading managers or experts and later, to leading leaders.

They described how coaching increased their self-awareness, helped overcome obstacles, and guided them in navigating office politics. Each transition required not only a shift in behaviors but also a different level of accountability. It took time and practice for these shifts to show their impact. Notably, none of the leaders spoke about negative coaching experiences what stood out were stories of resilience, challenges, and change.

Their experiences echo the findings of Clifton Longenecker and Mike McCartney in their 2019 research, *The Benefits of Executive Coaching:*

Voices from the C-Suite, highlighting how coaching helps senior leaders identify the behaviors needed at each stage of leadership. Through each transition, their ability to reflect on what's required in each new role becomes critical. But as Longenecker and McCartney pointed out, senior leaders often struggle to make time for reflection and self-assessment. An executive coach helps leaders make space for reflection and stay focused on their growth. When combined with 360-degree feedback, this process surfaces the behaviors that matter most in the moment. Without such clarity, progress slows, and leadership impact can diminish.

COACHING FOR MORE THAN A TITLE

Jason was a leader at a Fortune 500 technology firm specializing in productivity software, enterprise solutions, and cloud computing. The management offered him six coaching sessions as part of a leadership development initiative. I was chosen for the sessions, and in the last session, I asked if he now viewed coaching as a tool for leadership growth. He paused before saying, 'Well, it was certainly refreshing and gave me an outside-in perspective.'

Then, almost reflexively, he asked, 'So, after six sessions with a coach, am I a leader now?'

He didn't wait for an answer.

Instead, he continued with 'I think there's a bigger theme here. How can we coach leaders in the Senior Leadership Team? How are they modeling behaviors and demonstrating empathy for their teams?' He answered his own question: 'It'll take more than six sessions.'

As I listened to him, I thought of Marshall Goldsmith's philosophy on coaching, that the further we progress in our careers, the most meaningful changes we can make are behavioral, not functional.

I nodded to him. 'This sort of transformation does take time, and he agreed.

I often ask leaders, "How long do you think a coaching engagement should last?" I ask because it's one of the most common questions I receive. Most leaders say, "About a year," which matches with my own experience. When the focus is on behavioral change developing inclusive habits or navigating complex leadership challenges a year tends to be the minimum. Sustained change takes time, reflection, and the opportunity to practice new behaviors in real situations.

That said, if the coaching goal is more focused such as sharpening public speaking skills or developing a specific skill set, then five or six sessions may be enough. In those cases, success is typically measured by whether the goal is achieved, like delivering a great presentation.

In my coaching work with leaders on inclusion, I've found that behavioral change rarely happens overnight. It typically takes 9–18 months for new behaviors to take root. Visible results show up at the team level first, then in employee engagement or workplace culture surveys. Using a pre- and post-assessments, these changes can be tracked, challenging the notion that inclusion isn't measurable. Still, many organizations want immediate results. But inclusion and the leadership behaviors that support it require time, reflection, and reinforcement. This isn't about quick fixes. It's about embedding inclusive behaviors that match evolving organizational demands. That's what sustainable coaching delivers.

Throughout this book, I have shared both the tangible and intangible costs of non-inclusive leadership. In my interviews, I started with two central questions:

- What does inclusion mean to you?
- What impact does inclusion have on your organization?

Every leader responded positively to the question on the impact of inclusion, one in particular stood out. A founder of a start-up gaming company put it simply: *"I wouldn't have the business I have without the diversity of people, thinking, and backgrounds, our ability to connect across ideas and content is everything. Inclusion isn't just part of our culture; it defines both how we operate internally and how we engage with clients. It's who we are."*

INSIGHTS FROM LEADERS ON INCLUSION AND CHANGE

Continuing with that first "What does inclusion mean to you?" question, the head of client adoption and engagement at a global technology company in Singapore

We started by removing the DEI team.

With a shocked look on my face, trying not to judge this response, I pulled on Nancy Kline's listening practice and paused much longer than usual before asking, "What more would you like to think or say about inclusion?"

"We shifted to allyship, (supporting and advocating for colleagues from underrepresented group), and inclusion. Inclusion is key. It wasn't just theory; it was a shift in how we worked. We had conflict and there were definitely points of tension. But over time, the conflicts became productive, even honorable." She believed that for any organization working across 15 different markets in Asia Pacific, inclusion was not simply a strategy; it was the only way to understand the nuances of each market.

Asking the same question to the Managing Director of a global luxury brand she said, "For us, it wasn't only about diversity numbers; it was about creating a place where everyone, regardless of experience, background, or education, felt valued and heard. We started with a goal for inclusion, but over time, this became part of who we are. We have 50–50 gender representation across markets and leadership. We speak up, ask questions, and are comfortable with our own identity. This requires all of us to be deliberate in how we approach inclusion."

A finance leader at a global bank in Singapore responded with:

Diversity? Inclusion? Honestly, I hadn't given it much thought. It should come naturally, but it doesn't. I've worked around the world and felt it was my job to assimilate into the organization, not the other way around. I never expected the organization to adjust to my style. I wouldn't say I was excluded, but I was on the outside.

I never realized that organizations could be more flexible in creating space for different styles of leadership. Until you just asked, I believed I had to find a way to fit in without giving up who I am. I've learned to assimilate while also bringing others into the culture but need to earn trust by building relationships and showing respect.

Yet another finance leader shared a personal experience with me:

I had a boss who didn't like my style. When people talk about 'being who you are at work,' well, it didn't work for me. I sent out weekly emails to update colleagues on company happenings. My boss thought I was being too open. When we were together in Singapore, he pulled me aside and told me to just stop sending them. He said, 'It makes you look weak, and I need you to look the part.' Even though he asked me to stop, I kept sending them. And the truth is, I built strong relationships through those emails. Now that I think about it, isn't that what inclusion is all about?

Inclusion in Academic Institutions

Moving from business to academia, leaders in Asia are strengthening their commitment to inclusion. In Hong Kong I interviewed faculty members during a turbulent period; they described how universities in Hong Kong have expanded research funding, supported cross-disciplinary collaboration, and directed resources toward broader societal impact. A few faculty members described how their university was focusing more on inclusion, directing resources toward broader research fields, faculty collaboration and expanding grant access. One faculty in the School of Humanities in Hong Kong and another professor of Communications in Japan, said, "We've seen more innovative research projects and definitely more growth from expanding funding." Rather than pulling back on inclusion, universities take a more reflective approach, drawing on philosophy, history, and sociology to ask: *How do we shape more inclusive practices?*

While many Asian universities' mission statements emphasize ideals such as advancing human well-being, supporting open academic communities, or contributing to society through education and research, some are now taking practical steps to align with changing demographics and needs. In Japan and Australian universities have introduced dual-career support for academic couples, offered more flexible tenure policies, and launched career watch programs to support ongoing development. These efforts signal mark a broader shift from stated intentions to measurable inclusion. Higher education institutions are beginning to recognize the need to translate inclusive values into daily practice, not just aspiration.

In the United States, diversity, equity, and inclusion (DEI) initiatives in higher education are navigating an era of uncertainty. Growing political pushback, at both federal and state levels, has led to increased scrutiny, funding threats, and, in some cases, the rollback of DEI programs. These pressures have created a sense of risk for institutions, prompting some to slow down or reassess their efforts. As this landscape continues to evolve, the future of inclusive practices in U.S. higher education remains unsettled.

Inclusion in Religious Communities and NGOs

These two (seemingly disparate) communities both demonstrate a strong commitment to inclusion, not only as a stated value but as a daily practice embedded in interactions. In conversations with religious and NGO leaders, three common threads emerged: the role of storytelling, the practice of empathy, and the importance of reflection in creating inclusive spaces. For example, both Mennonite communities and NGOs use storytelling to deepen understanding and make sense of shared experiences.

In the Mennonite community, storytelling is central to weekly gatherings where individuals share personal experiences under the theme *"This is me."* Elders in the community explained that this practice draws on the Ghanaian concept of *Sankofa*, a word from the Akan language symbolized by a bird turning its head backward to retrieve an egg. *Sankofa* means "to go back and fetch it" an invitation to reclaim what has been forgotten, lost, or left behind in order to move forward with wisdom (Temple 2010). This philosophy echoes my inclusive coaching approach, where I invite leaders to reflect on pivotal career moments, not to dwell, but to uncover insight, and move ahead with clarity.

This practice of drawing on the past is echoed across interviews with leaders in faith communities, academia, and NGOs. They emphasized that inclusion requires engaging with history, learning from experience, and sitting with discomfort rather than avoiding it. One pastor spoke of using appreciative inquiry, an approach that encourages reflection and thoughtful dialogue. Another pastor described how admitting uncertainty and showing vulnerability helped build trust within their community. Inclusion, they stressed, isn't a sign on the door; it's a continuous process of listening and making room for others.

This same reflective practice appears in NGOs, though often adapted to suit organizational culture. At the World Bank, for example, storytelling circles were introduced as a leadership practice to strengthen team connection. Over time, however, they faded, as employees struggled to make time. Yet the power of storytelling lies not in its length, but in its intention. The Mennonite community shows that even a few minutes can make a difference. In a leadership session with teams from the World Bank, UNESCO, and the Asian Development Bank, we used a brief 2-minute storytelling exchange focused on personal values. Much like the "This is me" practice, it sparked unexpected conversations and moments of empathy, reminders that even short, intentional stories can shift perspectives.

Common Threads in Inclusive Leadership

Through my analysis of narratives, I've heard four common themes on how leaders approach inclusion, across religious communities, NGOs, academia, and corporations:

1. **Demonstrating Conviction:** Embedding inclusion into the daily rhythm of work through meetings, delegating responsibilities, onboarding, performance reviews, talent decisions, and leadership selection. Introducing 'career watch' programs to support emerging faculty.
2. **Showing what Inclusion looks like:** Acting inclusively without explicitly labeling themselves as "inclusive leaders' by demonstrating empathy, fairness, and respect through actions that positively impact people and outcomes.
3. **Practicing Empathy and Listening:** Across all settings, from spiritual communities to global NGOs, leaders described inclusion as an active, ongoing practice of listening. Through storytelling circles, appreciative inquiry, or dialogue with members, empathy is a common thread weaving through conversations.
4. **Bringing Others Along:** Integrating inclusion through coaching, mentoring, and peer learning circles. The practice storytelling, like "This is me," uncovers personal values and experiences that might otherwise remain invisible.

Inclusion as a Continuous Process

Inclusion is not static. Leaders have described it to me as an ongoing process, requiring continual reflection and adaptation. Some needed support in scaling inclusive practices and structuring initiatives that made inclusion tangible. Many found that taking small, deliberate steps was more effective than broad, sweeping changes.

A global sales leader at a leading enterprise technology company in Singapore mentioned, "We are a sales-driven organization. Failure is truly not an option. We have a few humble leaders, and inclusion brings out the best in all of us. Traditional leadership models work, but inclusive leadership requires a different mindset. It takes time and more listening. Honestly, we need to get better at that too. We started with a top-down approach, but inclusion needs to be part of how we work every day. It's not a process; belonging is the foundation of our best work, it's how we do business." Another leader in healthcare framed it this way: "People leave companies when they don't see a future for themselves, when they don't feel included, when they don't see themselves reflected in leadership. Exclusion, whether intentional or not, pushes people out."

THE CONNECTION BETWEEN INCLUSION AND BELONGING

The comment *"Belonging is the foundation of our best work"* stood out to me. Many leaders I've worked with have echoed this sentiment, reinforcing why inclusion matters. At a global telecom company in Singapore, leaders aimed to embed belonging and inclusion into their culture. At the same time, Singapore's Future Skills Framework identified inclusion as a skill needed for the future. Many of the leaders I've coached in Singapore are now actively developing and integrating inclusive behaviors to make this a reality in their workforce.

At a workshop on Inclusive Leadership in Singapore for the global telecoms firm participants shared personal stories about belonging. One participant talked about his time in the army. Unlike many of his peers, he hadn't attended elite schools and initially felt excluded.

> *We were all thrown together, we ate together, trained together. But I wasn't really part of the group until the Sergeant pulled me aside to help with a technical problem. I suggested a quick fix and it worked. From that point on, things changed. It's the same back at the office. Unless you're invited in, you're on the outside looking in.*

Their stories reinforced the idea that while belonging is important, it doesn't stand alone. It is the result of working for an inclusive leader. Everyone wants to feel a sense of belonging, but inclusion is what enables it.

Belonging is a feeling; inclusion is an action. When organizations focus on developing inclusive behaviors, belonging naturally grows.

How Do We Build Inclusive Leaders?

Coaching plays a key role in developing specific leadership behaviors.

The Managing Director of a global bank who had worked regionally partnered with a coach during each major career transition from a back-office individual contributor role to leading managers supporting the trade desk, and eventually to overseeing leaders across several functions. Coaching helped him adapt his leadership style, manage broader responsibilities, and build credibility with senior stakeholders. It wasn't just a shift in scope, but in how he led.

In interviews, a number of leaders described how coaching supported them at different levels from skill building and goal achievement to deeper self-awareness, overcoming hurdles, and shifting behaviors. One Singaporean leader at an American bank shared that coaching helped him read body language and understand when to speak up or step back. When he later moved to a British bank, he found the culture more consensus-driven and collaborative but struggled with being more direct. "Coaching helped me adapt while staying true to who I was as a leader."

These conversations echo David Clutterbuck and David Megginson's insight that *"a coaching culture is one where coaching is the predominant style of managing and working together, and where commitment to improving performance is embedded at every level."* While Longenecker and McCartney focused on aligning leadership behaviors through different stages of a leader's career. Clutterbuck and Megginson emphasize building a coaching culture, one that encourages dialogue, reflection, and learning across the organization. These practices also create the conditions in which inclusive leadership can take root. Their emphasis on generative conversations, where insight emerges through intentional listening, aligns with the inclusive coaching approaches explored throughout this book.

Coaching Levels and Their Impact

1. **Level 1: Instructional Coaching:** Bridging skills gaps, providing specific guidance and skills development. In Jason's story, six coaching sessions focused on short-term skill building, getting things done, and solving immediate challenges. But as Jason recognized, real transformation requires deeper work.

2. **Level 2: Developmental Coaching:** Focusing on personal growth, reflection, and leadership identity (Who do I want to be as a leader?). For Angelina, "this is where coaching became more powerful for me." Coaching helped her refine her leadership identity. "I started to see behavioral patterns that needed to change and learned how to move through the organizational culture more effectively."
3. **Level 3: Behavioral Shift Coaching:** Addressing leadership behaviors, self-awareness, and influence. The finance leader at a British bank struggled with balancing direct versus indirect communication styles. Coaching helped him navigate cultural expectations while staying aligned with his own leadership style. "This is where coaching really shaped me as a leader." "It wasn't just about skills; it was about how I engaged with others, how I built trust."

With coaching inclusive leaders, I spend most of my time at Level 3.

Coaching Works, but It Takes Time

Coaching is instrumental in building inclusive leadership skills. Inclusive leadership requires behavioral skills that don't come naturally. One leader stated that coaching provided tailored support which shaped his leadership style. "I worked on my own for a long time, trying to figure out my next step. When I finally landed a new role, I knew I needed a coach. That coaching relationship was invaluable, as it helped me see what I wasn't seeing and challenged me in ways I needed. One piece of feedback really stuck with me was 'that I could be more inclusive with few members on my team. I'd always prided myself on being fair, seeing the team as a whole when clearly this message wasn't getting through.'

His coaching experience was so impactful that he reflected on it in a personal article titled *"The Top Eight Things I Learned,"* which he shared with peers and colleagues. His first insight was that everything begins with trust, a perspective that resonates with David Maister's research on relationship-building. He wrote: *"It's more than making people feel safe. It's about genuinely caring about their growth, illustrating instead of instructing, and demonstrating that you've really listened."*

This emphasis on trust also echoes David Clutterbuck's view that it forms the foundation of effective coaching. In his book *Coaching the*

Team at Work (2007), he writes: *"Trust is the lubricant of coaching. Without it, the conversation grinds. With it, almost anything is possible."*
When coaching for inclusion, trust *is* the starting point. While working with leaders from a global luxury brand in Hong Kong, we began with one-on-one coaching sessions before moving into smaller peer learning groups. Sharing the results of a 360-assessment called for openness and humility. It also required care in how feedback was handled, what remained private and what individuals felt comfortable sharing with the group. Addressing these concerns helped create an environment where participants felt they could speak honestly about their strengths and challenges building an inclusive team culture.

Before the group sessions began, we co-created rules of engagement, agreements on how we wanted to work together, using a set of reflective questions to guide the discussion. We used an anonymous approach, asking questions such as: *"On a scale of 1 to 5, how much risk am I willing to take?"* and *"How much do I care about others in the room?"* These questions help to create an environment for honest dialogue laying the groundwork for trust, opening the way for appreciative feedback.

In addition to coaching, several leaders I interviewed mentioned the importance of peer learning groups or having a strong leader who both challenged and supported them over time. One executive described it like this:

> *Every manager I've had helped me grow, but one in particular would always say, 'Let's talk about you, not just your work.' That one sentence stuck with me; it changed how I approached leadership. My boss had a PhD in psychology, and I think that's what made him a better leader.*

While not every leader has an advanced degree in psychology, this reflection highlights how some bring an understanding of human dynamics into their leadership. For the people they support, it makes a lasting impact.

The Timeframe for Behavioral Change

One ongoing question is the duration of coaching, which I raised earlier, with most leaders suggesting about a year. But the debate is often for a short fix. There can often be a disconnect between HR's more structured coaching timelines and the reality of sustainable behavioral change.

A marketing leader working for a chemical company in China said, *"Some companies offer three-month coaching engagements, others nine months to a year. But real transformation? That takes time."*

Coaching for behavioral change shouldn't follow a rigid timeline; it needs to be flexible and responsive to a leader's evolving needs. During my time in Hong Kong as Head of Talent and Organizational Development at the Walt Disney Company, we found that short, targeted coaching was particularly useful for leaders transitioning into new roles, helping them adjust quickly to address immediate challenges. But when it came to shifting leadership behaviors, a longer-term approach was essential. For change to stick, it needs consistent reinforcement.

The popular myth that it takes just 21 days to form a new habit has been widely debunked (Robbins 2021). Research by Phillippa Lally et al. (2009), previously referenced, found that depending on the complexity of the behavior, it can take up to 254 days to internalize a new habit. The same holds true in leadership: lasting change requires sustained practice, feedback, and reinforcement. As one leader in a chemical company put it:

I had one session per week for about three months, then bi-weekly sessions for another nine weeks. After that we did a six-month check-in and an annual follow-up. Even then, I still found myself falling back into old habits. More time with the coach keeps holding you accountable.

In a conversation with a finance leader in Hong Kong, she said, "Project management skills? You can pick those up pretty quickly. But trying to be a leader… well, that's different." For her, coaching wasn't about a set number of sessions. The bottom line? Coaching works best when it follows the pace and priorities of a busy executive.

Measuring the Investment in Executive Coaching

Whether from the Chief Learning Officer, Chief Human Resource Officer, or Chief Executive Officer, persistent (and understandable) question is how to measure the impact of investment in coaching.

Given the cost of coaching, organisations should indeed want to measure expenditure vs effectiveness. The International Coaching Federation's (ICF) 2023 Global Coaching Study, conducted by PricewaterhouseCoopers (PwC), estimates that the global coaching industry generated approximately $4.564 billion USD in 2022, with over 109,000 active coach practitioners worldwide. Projections suggest that the industry could reach $7.3 billion USD by 2025. These figures are based on data collected from active coaching professionals.

Taking this one step further coaching fees vary across levels. According to Arden Coaching, hourly rates range from $200 to $3000 per hour. A comprehensive coaching engagement over a period of months can range from $5000 to $15,000, with more intensive programs reaching up to $30,000 for senior leaders. The variations depend on the coach's experience, the structure of the engagement, and the depth of services provided.

Despite the investment in coaching, some organizations still struggle with how to measure impact, often not because they don't value measurement, but because defining success can be more nuanced than expected. Different leaders have different ways of assessing progress, and in some cases, the challenge begins with vague goals at the outset.

I've researched the measurement of coaching for years, and it requires both a quantitative and qualitative approach, starting with clearly defined success metrics. At the beginning of an engagement, the first question should be, *"What would success look like at the end of the coaching?"* Not everyone has a definitive answer right away. A typical response I've heard is, *"I don't know, but I'll know when I get there."*

Some organizations use Anthony M. Grant's Well-being and Engagement Framework (WBEF), which explores how coaching impacts both well-being and engagement, defined as the sense of purpose, involvement, and energy an individual brings to their work. The four-quadrant model maps high vs. low well-being and low vs. high engagement, offering a structured way to assess early indicators of coaching effectiveness.

Others use platforms like BetterUp, which take a broader approach by tracking outcomes such as business performance, employee retention, and well-being metrics at scale. BetterUp's coaching platform evaluates a range of outcomes, offering organizations a data-driven way to align personal development with business goals.

Do these approaches work? Yes, particularly in large-scale environments where consistency and comparability matter. These frameworks offer structure and clarity, especially when measuring ROI across thousands of users. But in my practice, working closely with leaders inside organizations, impact is often most visible in the formal metrics: in the clarity a leader gains, the relationships they strengthen, and the decisions they shift as a result. Whether I use a 360 assessment or a set of reflection prompts, success begins with a conversation around goals and measurement flows from there.

Taking the long view to measurement means looking at how leadership behaviors evolve beyond the final coaching session. Yet many organizations are hesitant to conduct post-coaching evaluations, often citing time constraints or concerns about adding cost. In some cases, there's also a lack of internal structure or ownership around what happens after the coaching ends, particularly when a sponsor or leader changes roles, so follow-up falls off the radar.

In my own practice, post-coaching measurement is part of the process. This might include a follow-up 360, a short pulse survey, or a reflective conversation with the leader and their manager or HR team, 3–6 months later. These quick check-ins not only reinforce change, but offer insight into what shifted, and where to go next.

The Challenge of Measuring Too Quickly

A persistent challenge I've observed is the push to evaluate coaching impact too soon. Some organizations rely on quick feedback surveys, often referred to as "happy sheets" capturing immediate satisfaction but revealing little about behavioral change. Many leaders I've worked with emphasize the time needed to show impact:

> *Right after a program ends? That's the worst time to measure impact. You have to give people time to apply what they've learned. Maybe six months, maybe a year—that's when you see real change.*

This echoes Daniel Goleman's (2000) insight that one of the most critical leadership skills for building cohesive teams in the face of constant change doesn't come naturally, developing gradually with deliberate effort and sustained practice. That is one main reason why tracking leadership behaviors over time is non-negotiable.

Adding to Pre- and Post-assessments: Measuring Coaching Impact in Inclusive Leadership

In addition to traditional pre- and post-coaching assessments, two powerful approaches provide insight into coaching outcomes:' concept of Mutual Exchange and the practice of reflexivity.

Burns' Mutual Exchange framework emphasizes the use of both quantitative and qualitative data to understand coaching impact at both the individual and team levels. In working with several organizations, we applied this approach by combining 360 assessments (quantitative), stakeholder interviews (qualitative), and employee engagement surveys (both quantitative and qualitative).

For one client, we focused specifically on two inclusive leadership behaviors: participation and team unity. After the second ILC 360 assessment, leaders reviewed both their numerical scores and verbatim feedback from team members to reflect on how their behaviors had shifted. This blend of data provided a clearer picture of impact, not only through metrics, but through experiences of those around them. Learning to lead inclusively while delivering business results doesn't happen overnight. It takes practice.

A second way to assess coaching impact is through reflexivity, the intentional practice of self-reflection followed by adjustment. While reflection involves looking back and making sense of experiences, reflexivity is more immediate and active. It's about noticing in the moment, questioning one's assumptions, and making real-time shifts in behavior. As such, reflexivity is often described as "thought-in-action," rather than "thought-after-action." Let me add this isn't easy, it's a deliberate, conscious practice, similar to Chapter 5 when we discussed Schein's here-and-now humility.

The concept is explored in academic literature, especially in leadership education, coaching, and qualitative research. Researchers such as Margaret Archer and Linda Finlay have written extensively about reflexivity as a process of inner dialogue that informs action. In coaching contexts, reflexivity supports sustained change by preventing regression into old habits and reinforcing newly learned behaviors.

In my interviews, leaders who practiced reflexivity, pausing to assess their actions and recalibrate their approach experienced the most lasting impact from coaching. A finance leader mentioned, *"At first, I thought coaching was just about fixing little anomalies, but over time, I started asking myself: 'How am I showing up? And what's my impact on others?' This changed the way I lead."*

Coaching creates space for reflexivity, encouraging leaders to slow down and reconsider their approach, as discussed in Chapters. 3–5.

Reflexivity helps:

- Recognize blind spots and challenge one's thinking
- Adjust one's leadership style based on context and feedback
- Strengthen inclusive behaviors by remaining open to multiple perspectives

When paired with data-driven insights from tools like the Inclusive Leadership Compass (ILC) 360, leaders gain a fuller picture of how they're perceived and their impact on others. By integrating any one of the above methods, organizations move beyond surface-level metrics to capture the real value of coaching.

The head of creative content for a global entertainment firm shared, *"I block one day each month for deep thinking. No meetings. I sit down with a notebook and just write. Like Jack Kerouac's stream-of-consciousness writing, I fill three pages with whatever comes to mind. It's helped me understand myself better and, honestly, become a better leader. I call it my fountain pen bot session."*

That final comment about his "fountain pen bot session" led me to explore a new question:

What role will AI play in coaching and leadership development? One theme I heard in these interviews is that while human connection will likely remain central to leadership growth, the landscape is shifting. Many leaders shared stories of how digital tools including AI-powered chatbots are already supporting development at scale. I wanted to understand their perspective: Can AI deepen self-awareness? Can it reinforce inclusive behaviors?

As we close this chapter and look ahead, Otto Scharmer's message echoes throughout: *"The quality of results produced by any system depends on the quality of awareness from which people in the system operate."* Behavioral change requires reflection and self-awareness, not just skill acquisition. And meaningful measurement begins with insight and awareness from the people within the system itself.

In the next chapter, we explore how AI-powered tools are being used to support leadership development and where their limits may lie. As we enter that discussion, it is important to reflect on the human aspects of leadership. As you reflect on your own leadership, how do ethics, inclusion, and humanity shape your decisions? What commitments can you make to lead with a moral compass? We will carry these questions with us as we look at the role of AI in leadership development.

REFERENCES

Clutterbuck, D. (2007). *Coaching the team at work*. Nicholas Brealey Publishing.

Goleman, D. (2000). *Leadership that gets results*. Harvard Business Review, 78(2), 78–90.

Lally, P., Van Jaarsveld, C. H. M., Potts, H. W. W., & Wardle, J. (2009). How are habits formed: Modelling habit formation in the real world. *European Journal of Social Psychology, 40*(6), 998–1009. https://doi.org/10.1002/ejsp.674

Robbins, J. (2021, January 5). *How long does it really take to form a habit?* Scientific American. https://www.scientificamerican.com/article/how-long-does-it-really-take-to-form-a-habit/

Temple, C. N. (2010). Sankofa: Celebrating the past to awaken the future. *The Journal of Pan African Studies, 3*(10), 127–142.

CHAPTER 11

AI-Powered Tools for Coaching Inclusion

The future is not something you predict. The future is something you make.
Jane McGonigal

In the previous chapter, that final comment, "fountain pen bot session," led me to consider a different question: *What role can AI play in coaching and leadership development?* Admittedly this is a slippery slope, especially with technology evolving quickly but this question now surfaces often in my interviews and coaching conversations. With AI-powered chatbots used increasingly to support learning and development, it's necessary to discuss.

When I asked leaders about the Human vs. AI debate, one thread remained consistent: the human connection remains at the core of leadership growth. But there is also a widely shared recognition that the landscape is changing—very quickly.

Leaders described how digital tools, especially AI-powered platforms like ChatGPT, Gemini, and Rocky.AI, are beginning to scale multiple aspects of leadership development, from supporting reflection and communication practice to filtering data from assessments and offering personalized feedback. For simplicity, I use the term *"chatbot"* to refer to AI-powered platforms, which were the focus of my conversations with leaders. My three questions were:

- Can a chatbot support the development of self-awareness?
- Can it encourage inclusive behaviors?
- What are its possibilities, and where are its limits?

Responses were mixed at first, most insisted that no technology could replace the human element in coaching. But more recently, the responses changed:

Maybe a 20-year-old entering the workforce would engage with an AI coach more effectively than I would. I still believe real conversations and personal connection are irreplaceable.

The more seasoned executives highly valued the human connection and as I listened, I wondered more on the generational divide.

In academia, the divide appeared more pronounced. University professors widely acknowledged the growing use of tools like ChatGPT, and in Asia, DeepSeek as they both provide learning and writing support for students.

In response to my question about how chatbots might support coaching like behaviors, one professor offered this perspective: *"Students value chatbots because they offer a judgment-free space. They'll ask questions they might hesitate to ask a human mentor. Platforms like ChatGPT or DeepSeek can give feedback and learning prompts similar to coaching, right?"*

I agreed. When I asked further about this judgment-free space, the professor shared an example: a student working on a leadership paper received this response from a chatbot: *"You're absolutely on the right track with the message, but it could be refined slightly to sound more confident, polished, and grounded in leadership language."*

While some professors initially resisted the use of chatbots, many recognized it's nearly impossible to stop. As one professor put it, *"We tried to stop it, but it's impossible."* Rather than banning them, some faculty are now exploring how these tools can spark thinking particularly for students who are stuck or unsure how to begin. Several professors saw value in using chatbots for first drafts or brainstorming, recognizing their role in helping students to get started, rather than procrastinate on writing a paper.

One professor in Japan said, "AI has a role to play in development. It's how you use it… seek wisdom from AI." He told me, "I suggested to my students that they set up a dialogue between two different leaders from history and have them argue about a business question. One student chose Napoleon and a Zen Master." He paused and smiled. "The exchange was... unexpectedly insightful." He finished with, "It would be naïve not to think AI will be a valuable emotive tool for support.

In my coaching practice, I've tested a number of AI-powered tools like Gemini, ChatGPT, and Rocky.AI. These tools not only offer a neutral space for exploration, but their use of positive reinforcement promotes a slightly more encouraging learning experience. They constantly provide subtle, positive feedback.

When I asked ChatGPT for an example of feedback during a client meeting, it responded: *"Great job staying focused and asking thoughtful follow-up questions. You helped build trust and kept the conversation productive."* Yes, it's scripted, but it offers the kind of affirmation that many users find encouraging, somewhat to their chagrin, but are becoming more and more comfortable with such interactions. ChatGPT and Gemini function as versatile conversational agents, while Rocky.AI provides more structured coaching prompts tailored to individual development.

Another professor suggested that using chatbots in coaching wasn't just viable, but necessary: *"For the next generation, AI fits. You can use the same coaching principles, but the medium needs to evolve. If a chatbot helps them engage and learn, why not use it?"*

Not all agree. For obvious reasons.

Business executives were more cautious. A finance leader in tax strategy put it bluntly: *"90% of my work can be done by AI. Bots can handle tax hurdles, calculations, and strategic modeling. But can they really help change behaviors? Maybe. I don't know."*

Others were more optimistic: *"Chatbots can fill some gaps. They help with skill-building, offer reminders, and support interpersonal growth. Not everyone has time for frequent coaching sessions. Plus, it's a really compelling product."*

As public access to AI tools expanded in 2022, research into AI in coaching grew. In their 2025 article, *"AI Coaching: Democratising Coaching or Offering an Ersatz?"*, Tatiana Bachkirova and Rob Kemp argue that AI lacks the depth of reflection and adaptive judgment required for meaningful growth. "AI cannot replicate the depth of introspection, or the flexibility required for true reflexivity," they wrote. They also noted that AI falls short in cultural, historical, and contextual awareness.

While I reference this research, my aim in this chapter isn't to provide a comprehensive academic review. No doubt, the field will continue to evolve. What matters is how leaders are engaging with these tools today and what possibilities (and limitations) they're noticing in real time.

Using the International Coaching Federation's definition of coaching as a partnership, Bachkirova and Kemp proposed that a better term might be "joint inquiry," as it captures the dialogic, mutual nature of the coaching process. In contrast, AI lacks personal awareness, cannot draw from lived experience, and only mimics empathy without genuine emotional understanding.

While it may offer pre-programmed prompts or simulations, it cannot recognize, adapt in the moment nor reflect the emotional nuances in face-to-face coaching. Still, the authors recognize AI's value in areas such as data analysis, real-time feedback, and self-directed goal setting, particularly when paired with metrics which track individual progress.

This is consistent with what I'd heard in my interviews, where leaders suggested a hybrid approach. *"A chatbot can nudge, but can it interpret body language? A human coach picks up on those unconscious cues in tone, posture, hesitation. A chatbot might offer guidance, but a coach helps refine your message and strengthen emotional intelligence."*

Bachkirova and Kemp also emphasized that AI's strongest contribution is to improve access to coaching, making it available to more people, more often, which I also heard echoed by business leaders. That said, skepticism remains. The authors concluded that current AI-based coaching tools don't meet six essential criteria that define organizational coaching: relationship building, ethical awareness, reflective practice, contextual sensitivity, learning facilitation, and development focus. These areas require empathy, contextual understanding, and adaptability. Qualities that AI has yet learned to fully replicate.

I'll also add that for David Clutterbuck's coaching levels, AI may be well suited to Level 1 and Level 2 engagements, offering reflection, structure, and behavioral nudges. Level 3, which requires deeper insight and transformation, still benefits from human intervention.

Emerging Tools Reshaping the Landscape

There are many AI-powered platforms rapidly reshaping how coaching is delivered. While each tool has its own strengths, the aim is to make coaching more accessible and scalable. I engaged directly with one of them, Rocky.AI, and explored AIMY through available research and practitioner insight.

Oddly enough, Rocky.AI sent me a nudge this morning, reminding me to stay positive about a goal. A well-timed nudge, since that goal is this book.

What follows is a brief look at two tools, starting with AIMY by CoachHub, an AI-driven coach offering real-time, interactive experiences tailored to individual goals.

AIMY by CoachHub is an AI-driven coach offering real-time, interactive experiences tailored to individual goals.

- Pros:
  AIMY guides users through skill-building exercises, provides instant feedback, and helps track progress over time. AIMY personalizes the coaching experience based on user input and reinforces behavior through repetition. Its 24/7 availability makes it a convenient tool for ongoing development.
- Cons:
  As Bachkirova and Kemp's research highlights, AIMY lacks the nuance and emotional insight of a human coach. Conversations can feel scripted, emotional shifts are often stilted, and contextual or cross-cultural understanding is largely absent.

Rocky.AI takes a different approach, offering short, daily coaching sessions focused on self-reflection, personal growth, and habit-building through brief, consistent engagement.

- Pros:
  Rocky.AI provides prompts, encourages accountability, and tracks progress. I've used it and found it helpful for daily nudges and staying focused on personal goals. It's especially useful for light reflection and maintaining momentum.
- Cons:
  Interacting with Rocky.AI, the prompts can feel generic or overly scripted, and at times I ignored notification. Rocky.AI doesn't yet reach the depth required for what David Clutterbuck calls Level 3 Coaching, work that involves sustained behavioral change, this

requires a level of adaptive, human responsiveness that no doubt AI tools are evolving toward.

While both are excellent supplements, at present neither are replacements for a live coaching relationship.

One leader who used Rocky.AI shared that: *"It's useful for structured reflection. The system prompts me with focused questions and helps me stay on track. But would I replace human coaching with AI? No. AI complements coaching, it doesn't replace it."*

WHERE AI COACHING WORKS AND WHERE IT FALLS SHORT

Leaders recognize both the value and limitations of AI coaching. Tools like AIMY and Rocky.AI provide positive nudges to support learning goals, particularly when a coach isn't available. For example, ChatGPT offers suggestions on improving listening skills or giving feedback, but lacks the subtle empathy of a coach, when a client expresses frustration or hesitation. A coach might pause, explore the emotional undercurrent and respond in the moment with care. AI, by contrast, may very well miss such signals.

There are clear boundaries to what AI can offer. It can't detect vocal tone, body language, or "read between the lines" the way a skilled coach can. These limitations aren't just functional, they're ethical. AI systems are trained on data that reflects human decisions, norms, and biases. As Orly Lobel notes in *The Equality Machine*, a point I'll return to later in this chapter, bias in AI is real but not irreversible. With thoughtful design, testing, and inclusive oversight, she argues, AI can actually help detect and correct bias faster than humans.

Others take a more cautionary stance. In *Weapons of Math Destruction*, Cathie O'Neil warns that when left unchecked, algorithms can reinforce inequality under the illusion of objectivity, particularly in areas like hiring, credit scoring, and performance evaluation. The point is not that AI is inherently harmful, but that it mirrors the systems that shape it. A chatbot may unintentionally reinforce dominant cultural norms or miss the subtleties of power dynamics. Without the relational intelligence of a coach, it can't offer the same depth, adaptability, or context-specific insight that human-led coaching provides.

One leader had a story on this specific issue. After receiving feedback from her boss to "speak up more" in meetings, she did exactly that, only to hear that some colleagues perceived it as "too aggressive." She was also experimenting with an AI coaching tool, which sent weekly prompts, encouraging her to "use your voice" and "speak with confidence." The chatbot, unaware of the organizational context, continued sending reminders, unable to detect the complexity of her environment or power dynamics of the situation. The chatbot's advice was well intentioned and aligned with her coaching goals but lacked the sensitivity that the situation required.

The Bottom Line: A Hybrid Future for Coaching

The likely future of coaching is hybrid. AI tools will continue to evolve and play a significant supporting role, making coaching more accessible and consistent. But it's unlikely AI will replace human coaches. One CEO said that: *"AI helps us identify trends, but metrics alone don't drive inclusion. It's the decisions we make and the conversations we have that move the dial."*

As AI advances, human oversight remains essential. Coaches and organizations must stay involved to uphold ethical standards and ensure that the coaching process remains rooted in trust. In practical terms, AI will contribute to inclusive leadership development.

For example, by using a chatbot aligned with the Inclusive Leadership Compass, a leader could receive behavioral nudges related to openness, respect, participation, or facilitation, delivered daily, weekly, or monthly. While a nudge won't replace peer learning, mentors, or coaches, they can reinforce inclusive behaviors through ongoing reminders in between sessions, using data from assessments to design specific actions for development.

These conversations reflect a broader trend. According to a 2024 ICF Technology in Coaching Survey, 64% of coaches have experimented with AI tools to support client reflection and goal setting, though only 12% believe these tools can replace live sessions. This skepticism isn't surprising. For many coaches, AI is viewed less as a threat to their livelihood and more as a tool to extend their impact between sessions or reach clients who might otherwise not have access to coaching. Still, concerns remain. A 2025 McKinsey report noted that while AI tools are increasingly being adopted for leadership training, issues like bias and emotional accuracy remain top priorities for implementation teams.

LOOKING AHEAD: THE EVOLVING NATURE OF AI COACHING

As AI tools become more embedded in coaching, ethical questions arise. No longer rhetorical these questions demand attention. Data privacy, bias, transparency, and emotional safety now sit atop of the agenda in the evolving coaching landscape.

The International Coaching Federation (ICF) emphasizes confidentiality, consent, and trust as the structural pillars of the coaching relationship. As AI platforms are developed and deployed, they must be intentionally designed to uphold these principles. I've heard questions (and concerns) over *who owns the data? How is it stored? Who else sees it?* These are all practical concerns, challenging the very foundation of trust and confidentiality in coaching.

Bias remains another concern, as AI is only as inclusive as the data it's trained on. In *The Equality Machine*, Orly Lobel advocates for a future where technology is not feared but refined, used deliberately to detect and dismantle bias. She offers a compelling case that unlike humans, AI has the capacity to recognize patterns of exclusion more quickly and consistently *if* the system is designed with that goal in mind. The bright side that she mentions is that 'the scientific community has been making great strides in understanding algorithmic bias and discrimination and in teaching algorithms to detect, measure and mitigate these biases.'

One necessary initial step is to ask what voices are missing from the data? Many AI models are built on Western, English-language sources that fail to capture the realities of diverse communities. Some governments restrict data access altogether, limiting what models can learn. And so the very foundation of the AI's "knowledge" may be incomplete or skewed.

This gap becomes a reality in coaching conversations. This has the potential to impact inclusive coaching, where a nuanced understanding of identity, power, and context is essential. A chatbot might suggest "Speak up more in meetings" or "Be more confident" without recognizing that such advice, while well-intentioned, may not land the same way across different cultural or organizational contexts. In some environments, a direct communication style is preferred. In others, it may run counter to team norms and has the potential to *derail careers* by promoting behaviors that are misaligned with the cultural context or workplace reality.

This insight draws directly from my research, published in *Words Collide, Mindsets Remain: A Journey of Narrative Inquiry* (2013), which describes how language and its meaning change across cultures. Words we assume are universally understood, such as confidence, ambition or presence, often carry a more layered, context-specific connotations. "Confidence," for instance, may signal self-assurance in one culture and arrogance in another. Without contextual awareness, even well-designed AI can misfire.

But the challenges aren't limited to language or bias, they also extend to emotional safety. Unlike coaches, AI doesn't pick up on subtlety: a long pause, a shaky voice, or a change in posture that signals vulnerability. A coach might pause and ask, "You seem a bit reluctant to answer that question, what more are you thinking?" An AI system might respond with a scripted productivity tip like, *"If you're feeling stuck, try breaking the task into smaller chunks."* The response might confuse or result in a frustrated "What?" as chatbots miss the emotional undercurrents. When subtle cues are overlooked and the complexity of human experience gets reduced to bullet-point solutions, the coaching interaction becomes transactional, off-putting or at times, just boring.

This isn't simply a technical shortcoming; it's relational. Emotional safety isn't just a "nice to have" in coaching; it provides an avenue for truth-telling, experimentation, and growth. Ignoring it reduces coaching to prescribed outputs, removing the reflective space that makes it powerful.

The challenge isn't only an algorithmic bias; it's how we choose to regulate such technology. Consent is an issue, as users interact with coaching bots without knowing how their data will be used, who will access it, or how long it will be stored. Data collection remains an ethical and regulatory challenge in AI coaching. Because these systems often function as a *black box*, it's unclear how information is collected or used, making it difficult for users to give truly informed consent, which in turn breeds' mistrust. Whether the AI tool is introduced by the coach or mandated by the organization, coachees must be informed. They need to know what the tool does, how their data will be treated and that they can opt out, without fear or consequences.

These limitations don't negate the potential of AI in coaching, but they demand we proceed with care, reflection and intention. As technology continues to evolve, we must evolve with it, not just in capability, but in awareness and responsibility.

As I write this, AI chatbots continue to generatively learn at the speed of light. By the time this book is published, we may very well be operating in a different setting, one where many of the limitations mentioned above are no longer barriers. What feels mechanical now may soon feel intuitive. What lacks nuance today could be more contextualised tomorrow. The very nature of AI is to evolve. That's the dual nature of AI in coaching: it offers extraordinary promise and demands extraordinary responsibility. It's not one or the other, it's about designing a future where both coexist, ethically, inclusively and in service of growth.

We're already seeing early glimpses of that future. Tools like AIMY, Rocky.AI, and other platforms offer bite-sized nudges, reflective prompts and guided pathways to help users build habits and track progress. Such tools continuously learn through feedback loops and user interactions. With each iteration, they become more responsive, more personalized and more empathetic. Who's to say the cons listed above won't soon become pros?

I could list more platforms, but the truth is that everything is in motion. What's available today may look radically different tomorrow. The point isn't to catalog tools, it's to pay attention to how they're being shaped, who is shaping them and for whom they are being shaped. These questions address the concerns of ethics and inclusion.

That is why I hesitate to draw final conclusions. I hold firmly to the importance of human connection in coaching and the role of empathy and humanity in leadership. But as futurist Jane McGonigal reminds us *"The future is not something you predict. The future is something you make."* Her words tell us to stay curious and remain open, as AI moves the boundaries of possibility in ways we cannot yet fully imagine. Rather than framing the future as a choice between human and AI, the more important question is: how will we evolve and adapt together?

So what now? In the next (and final) chapter, we pull it all together—coaching, inclusion, and all the questions asked in each chapter.

I call it: *Not a Quick Fix, but all the questions in between.*

Conclusion: Empowering Change—Coaching for an Inclusive Future

We're at the end (of the book). I'd like to offer a short recap of the questions and practices for building inclusion. While every aspect of inclusive leadership matters, three themes emerged surfaced over and over again: self-awareness, empathy and humility.

None of these are hard skills to master, they are ways of being, of seeing and listening. They emerge in how you lead, how you coach and how you include others. At their core is one resolute practice: reflection.

That's not a navel gazing comment.

Reflection allows us to pause and listen, generatively. Not only with other people, but with yourself. As Nancy Kline writes in the Thinking Environment, such listening requires

- Attention: Allowing the story to go where it needs to go
- Equality: Treating others as peers, with no hierarchy
- Appreciation: Seeing what is good and saying so
- Difference: Committing to the freedom from untrue assumptions
- Place: Creating an environment that says *you matter here*

Reflection is the precursor to humility; what Edgar Schein calls the *here and now humility*. It's not knowing less but recognizing what we don't actually know. It grounds us when we're new to a team or when someone new joins our team. It lets us learn from anyone, at any level, in any role.

It's where self-awareness begins, answering that quiet question: *Who do I want to be as a leader?*

Scaled back, that question becomes *Who am I?* which draws from Eastern and Western inquiry and shows us how to lead intentionally. Not by what we *do*, but by how we *are*.

Inclusive leadership isn't fixed, but rather shaped by all the choices we've made, which necessitate additional reflection. Throughout this book, using the Inclusive Leadership Compass Framework, I've provided questions and shared the Thinking Environment process, one I've used for years to coach leaders, managers, individual contributors and fellow coaches.

Before we turn to the condensed list of questions aligned with the framework, let me end with an excerpt from Rainer Maria Rilke's poem, the *Book of Hours*. Rilke writes of an invisible current that runs through our lives, questions we carry long before we can answer them. His words are a reminder that inclusion isn't something we master. It's something we notice that we return to, from which we grow.

Each mind fabricates itself.
We sense its limits, for we have made them.
And just when we would flee them, you come
and make of yourself an offering.

This is, to me, the heart of inclusion, challenging us to let go of mental models and assumptions that shape how we view others.

- To become aware that our minds fabricate limits, on ourselves and others
- To listen from multiple sources and get perspectives which stretch and question our thinking
- To see people as valid in their own right without categorizing or credentialing

That is how leading with inclusion looks.

Let's turn to the questions, a reflective guidepost for oneself, others, teams, and organizations.

Not a Quick Fix: Questions That Shape Inclusive Leadership

What follows is a list of questions from every chapter, questions that filled the spaces between insight and action, that prod and tug you back to what matters. Use them as prompts, not prescriptions, as invitations rather than conclusions. Revisit them often as a quiet check-in, or weave them into your coaching practice, a chatbot, or a journaling rhythm to bring inclusiveness into everyday work.

Self: Reflecting Who You Are as a Leader
(Chapter 2: The Hidden Costs of Exclusion)

- Are you coaching others on inclusion, or keeping it to yourself?
- What inclusive practices do you want most for your organization, and what first steps can you take to champion them?
- How might these practices improve your work, your team's, and the business overall?
- Would the impact of these changes be noticeable, and where?

Self-Awareness and Conviction
(Chapter 3: The Inclusive Leadership Compass Framework)

- Who do you want to become?
- How does your leadership style intersect with inclusive behaviors?
- What obstacles might hinder your progress toward becoming a more inclusive leader?
- What support would help you strengthen your inclusive leadership?

End of Day Reflection Prompts
- Could you have approached any of today's situations differently?
- How did your actions affect others emotionally?
- Were there highs and lows today, and what was the impact on you and others?

Empathy and Teams
(Chapter 4: Empathy in Action: Leading Inclusive Teams)

Reflecting on Readiness for Coaching
- Are you ready to peel back the layers of self and reflect honestly?
- Are you willing to do the work, committing time and effort to change?
- Are you able to accept feedback and use it for personal growth?

Unpacking Perfectionism
- When do you find yourself most absorbed in work?
- When you are deeply engaged at work, how does perfectionism show up?
- How has the goal of excellence contributed to or detracted from outcomes and your team's well-being?
- What might change if you applied the 80/20 rule to your projects?
- What could you do to challenge perfectionist tendencies, drawing from times when imperfection led to unexpected positives?

Moving from Task to Empathy
- What about this project has been most challenging for you, and how has it affected you personally?
- If we could change one thing about how we work, what would it be and how would it help?
- What support would help you feel more successful and engaged?
- When was the last time you considered quitting, and what would have made a difference?

Building Connections by Bridging Structural Gaps
(Chapter 5: Leading with Humility)

Reflecting on Your Network
1. **Evaluate Network Structure**
    - Where are the gaps in expertise, function, or level across your network?
2. **Leverage and Connect**

- Who are the key stakeholders you need to align with beyond your immediate connections?

3. **Strategize and Diversify**
    - Whose perspectives or expertise are you missing, and where might you need to learn from others?

4. **Plan for a Strategic Network**
    - How can you step outside your comfort zone to build relationships that connect across the broader organization?

Unpacking Perceptions
- What do you want others to remember about working with you?
- Where might there be gaps between how you see yourself and how others see you?
- How can you make your intentions clearer through your interactions?

Onboarding and Talent Management
(Chapter 6: Addressing Inclusion Gaps in Organizational Systems and Processes)

Reflecting on Listening and Thinking Councils (Nancy Kline's Influence)
- When are you truly listening without interruption or judgment?
- What assumptions might you be making in this conversation?
- How can you create more space for others' independent thinking?
- How does your meeting structure either encourage or limit real thinking?

Reflecting on Onboarding and Developing Key Relationships A simple redesign of onboarding can address early gaps by creating a more integrated, holistic approach. This includes:

- Facilitating cross-functional introductions.
- Providing structured time to meet with key stakeholders and decision-makers.

- Offering guidance on mapping informal interconnections.
- Creating a visual map of relationships and information flow (ONA or manual mapping).
- Maintaining regular touch points during onboarding.
- Understanding the internal and external marketplace.

When Building New Relationships, Consider Asking

- How long have they been with the organization?
- What do they do, and how does it connect to your work?
- What does success look like for them — and for the organization?
- What are the biggest challenges they see ahead?
- Where are the opportunities?
- What needs to happen to build on these opportunities?
- What are their current priorities?
- What advice would they offer you as you begin?

Reflecting on Inclusive Meeting Practices

- Are you starting meetings by clarifying the purpose and outcome?
- Are you framing topics as open questions to invite thinking?
- Are you creating a space for real listening without interruptions?
- Are you reinforcing positive feedback before offering advice or suggestions?

Reflecting on Inclusive Talent Management

- What leadership behaviors do you value in this organization, and are they measurable?
- How does your onboarding process help new employees feel connected and valued?
- Who in your team might be excluded from decision-making, and what can you do to bring them in?
- When you listen, are you focused on understanding or preparing your response?
- How are you defining successful leadership, and do you recognize different leadership styles?

- How do you encourage constructive dialogue across different groups, and do others see it?

Career Conversations at Mid and Later Career Stages + Dual Career Couples (Chapters 7 and 8)

Reflecting on Career Conversations
- How do you define career success for yourself, and how has that definition evolved over time?
- Who else would you like to add to your network as a thought partner?
- If you left the firm tomorrow, what would you regret not doing?
- How would you describe your strengths?
- What gives you energy in your job?
- What strengths do you see in others that you would like to develop?
- Looking back, what have been your greatest career achievements?
- If you could never fail, what career would you explore?
- What are you looking forward to this year?
- If you were to teach, what subject would it be?
- What assumptions might be getting in the way of an important conversation?

Adaptive Career Coaching Approach Frame the conversation to deepen career insight:

- What uncertainties might the person be facing?
- What assumptions might they be holding onto?
- What do they need clarity on?

Pause and allow time for reflection.
Circle back to the core theme:

The real challenge is... [insert their words]. Does that feel accurate to you?

Follow emerging patterns rather than rushing to solutions.
Use reflective listening:

So what I'm hearing is...

Hold space for deeper thinking by asking:

What more would you like to think or say about this?

Reflecting on Dual-Career Conversations
- What does career success look like for each of us individually and together?
- What are our non-negotiables in this next career move?
- How do our strengths and interests complement each other?
- What constraints (e.g., visas, timing) need to be considered?
- How will we communicate openly about compromises and priorities?
- What support systems can we lean on during transitions?
- How do we make sure both careers stay visible and valued?

Supporting Dual-Career Conversations in Organizations Organizations can:

- Establish Dual-Career Coaching Teams to support career navigation and networking.
- Engage Career Coaches skilled in working with dual-career couples.
- Build cross-company networks to expand career opportunities.
- Promote open discussions about dual-career needs in recruitment and career conversations.

Inclusion means taking an expansive view of careers and recognizing shifts in the marketplace.

Exploring Career Choices: The ICCS Framework (Intelligent Career Card System)
- **Knowing Why:** What values and motivations are most important to my career choices?
- **Knowing How:** What skills and experiences do I want to build or strengthen?
- **Knowing Whom:** Who are the key relationships and networks that will help me move forward?

Organizational Change and Inclusion
(Chapter 9: Building Sustainable Inclusion Through Culture Change)

Starting the Conversation
- What does inclusion mean to you?
- What does it feel like to be excluded?

Framing Organizational Change
- As leaders, what do we stand for?
- What changes do we need—not just want—to make in our factories, and why?
- How will we turn these ideas into action?

Moving from Ideas to Action (Small Group Work)
- Who's involved?
- What's the specific action?
- When do we check in with one another?
- How will we measure our impact?

Embedding Inclusive Mindsets
- What does an inclusive meeting look like?
- If we approached problems inclusively, how would our solutions be different?
- What might get in our way of achieving this change?

Facilitating Insight with the Thinking Council Process:
(Adapted from Nancy Kline's Thinking Environment)
1. **Framing the Challenge:** Identify the core challenge and why it matters.
2. **Crafting the Right Question:** Create a question that guides deeper thinking.
3. **Clarifying Understanding:** Confirm that everyone understands the real issue.

4. **Silent Reflection:** Allow space for initial thoughts to surface without rushing.
5. **Thinking Rounds:** Use questions that help others think more clearly, rather than solve too soon.
6. **Checking for New Insights:** Surface new perspectives or options.
7. **Closing with Appreciation:** Highlight strengths or contributions noticed during the process.

Measuring Organizational Change and Inclusion

- **Baseline Assessment:** How are you assessing inclusion today? What behaviors are you tracking?
- **Time-Based Tracking:** How are you reinforcing and checking progress over time?
- **Multi-Method Measurement:** What data sources (behavioral assessments, pulse surveys, observations, feedback) are you using to capture progress?
- **Impact Analysis:** What insights emerge when you compare across teams or factories?
- **Action and Reinforcement:** How are you using the data to shape leadership development and sustain change?

Common Threads in Inclusive Leadership
(Chapter 10: Leaders' Perspectives on Inclusion, Coaching, and AI)

Questions Asked to Leaders

- How do you build inclusive leaders?
- What impact does inclusion have on your organization?
- How do you measure the impact of coaching?
- What is the right time to measure coaching impact?
- What tools should you use to evaluate inclusive leadership growth?

Common Themes in Inclusive Leadership
1. **Demonstrating Conviction:**

Embedding inclusion into the daily rhythm of work—through meetings, delegating responsibilities, onboarding, performance reviews, talent decisions, and leadership selection.
2. **Showing What Inclusion Looks Like:**
Acting inclusively without labeling themselves as "inclusive leaders," but consistently demonstrating empathy, fairness, and respect through everyday actions.
3. **Practicing Empathy and Listening:**
Describing inclusion as an active, ongoing practice of deep listening—through storytelling circles, appreciative inquiry, and open dialogue.
4. **Bringing Others Along:**
Integrating inclusion through coaching, mentoring, and peer learning circles. Storytelling exercises like "This is me" uncover personal values and hidden experiences.

Coaching Practice Insight: A Practical Approach to Measuring Change

- Take the long view: At the start of any coaching engagement, define what success looks like for both the individual and the organization.
- Use pre- and post-assessments (such as the Inclusive Leadership Compass or other data-driven tools) to capture behavioral shifts over time.
- Conduct qualitative stakeholder interviews to gather real-world feedback on leadership behavior and team dynamics.

This dual approach balances quantitative and qualitative data, helping organizations track progress and build sustainable change.

Final Reflection Questions
- How do ethics, inclusion, and humanity shape your decisions?
- What commitment can you make to lead with a moral compass?

Coaching in the Age of AI-Powered Tools
(Chapter 11: AI-Powered Tools for Coaching Inclusion)

Key Questions for Leaders and Coaches
- What role can AI play in coaching and leadership development?
- Can AI support self-awareness and inclusive behaviors?
- What are the possibilities and limits of AI-powered coaching?
- How do you ensure emotional safety, trust, and ethical practices when using AI?
- How might cultural context and bias impact AI-supported coaching conversations?

Coaching Practice Insight
- Take a hybrid approach: combine AI tools with human coaching to extend impact between sessions, not replace it.
- Emphasize the human connection: AI can nudge reflection, but human coaches are critical for deep, emotional, and contextual conversations.
- Proceed thoughtfully: ensure transparency about how data is used and how bias is detected and addressed.

Where AI Coaching Supports Growth
- Nudging and reinforcing learning habits.
- Expanding access to coaching support.
- Offering low-risk spaces for early self-reflection.

Where AI Coaching Falls Short
- Reading emotional cues like tone, hesitation, or posture.
- Adapting to cultural and contextual nuances.
- Building relational trust and psychological safety.

Coaching with AI: Key Takeaways
- AI can extend coaching through nudges and reflective prompts but cannot replace human emotional intelligence.

- According to the ICF Technology in Coaching Survey (2024), 64% of coaches have experimented with AI tools, but only 12% believe these tools can replace live coaching sessions.
- Emotional safety, trust, and contextual sensitivity remain uniquely human strengths.
- Ethical concerns like data privacy, bias detection, and cultural awareness must guide AI tool use.

References

Allocco, B., Lovich, D., Russell, M. S., & Brooks Taplett, F. (2018). *Making the workplace work for dual-career couples.* Boston Consulting Group.

Archer, M. S. (2007). *Making Our Way Through the World: Human Reflexivity and Social Mobility.* Cambridge University Press.

Arthur, M. B., Khapova, S. N., & Richardson, J. (2017). *An intelligent career: Taking ownership of your work and your life.* Oxford University Press.

Bachkirova, T., & Kemp, R. (2023). AI coaching: Democratising coaching or offering an ersatz? *Coaching: An International Journal of Theory, Research and Practice, 16*(1), 4–18. https://doi.org/10.1080/17521882.2022.2128875

Baggio, A., Digentiki, E., & Varma, R. (2019, October 7). *Organizations do not change—people do.* McKinsey & Company. https://www.mckinsey.com/capabilities/people-and-organizational-performance/our-insights/the-organization-blog/organizations-do-not-change-people-change

Beal, D., Benayad, A., & Newsom Reeves, K. (2023, October 16). *Banks can deliver both social impact and profits. Here's how.* Boston Consulting Group. https://www.bcg.com/publications/2023/balancing-social-impact-and-profits-with-banking

Boyatzis, R. E., Liu, H., Smith, A., Zwygart, K., & Quinn, J. (2024). Competencies of coaches that predict client behavior change. *The Journal of Applied Behavioral Science, 60*(1), 19–49. evidencebasedmentoring.org+1peopledevelopmentinstitute.org+1

Burns, J. M. (1978). *Leadership.* Harper & Row.

Burt, R. S. (1998). The gender of social capital. *Rationality and Society, 10*(1), 5–46. https://doi.org/10.1177/104346398010001001

Burt, R. S. (1992). *Structural Holes: The Social Structure of Competition*. Harvard University Press.
Benson, B. (2016, September 1). Cognitive bias cheat sheet: 4 conundrums of intelligence. Medium. https://medium.com/thinking-is-hard/4-conundrums-of-intelligence-2ab78d90740f
Carboni, I., Parker, A., & Langowitz, N. S. (2021). Mapping exclusion in the organization. MIT Sloan Management Review. https://sloanreview.mit.edu/article/mapping-exclusion-in-the-organization/
Catalyst. (2020, August 20). *Why diversity and inclusion matter: Quick take.* https://www.catalyst.org/insights/2020/why-diversity-and-inclusion-matter
Cheung, F. M., & Halpern, D. F. (2008). *Women at the top: Powerful leaders tell us how to combine work and family*. Oxford University Press.
Clarke, M. (2015). Dual careers: The new norm for Gen Y professionals? Career Development International, 20(6), 562–582. https://doi.org/10.1108/CDI-10-2014-0143
Clutterbuck, D. (2007). *Coaching the team at work*. Nicholas Brealey Publishing.
Clutterbuck, D., & Megginson, D. (2005). *Making coaching work: Creating a coaching culture*. Chartered Institute of Personnel and Development.
CoachHub. (n.d.). *AIMY: AI-powered coaching assistant*. Retrieved April 1, 2025, from https://www.coachhub.com/
Cognitive Talent Solutions. (2024, September 28). *Reducing employee attrition with ONA: A case study from a European IT company*. https://www.cognitivetalentsolutions.com/portfolio/reducing-employee-attrition-with-ona-a-case-study-from-a-european-it-company/
Development Dimensions International. (2023, March 7). *Women in leadership: Latest research and statistics*. DDI. https://www.ddiworld.com/blog/women-leadership-statistics
DeWall, C. N., Baumeister, R. F., & Vohs, K. D. (2010). Alone but feeling no pain: Effects of social exclusion on physical pain tolerance and pain threshold, affective forecasting, and interpersonal empathy. Journal of Personality and Social Psychology, 98(6), 886–899. https://scholars.uky.edu/en/publications/alone-but-feeling-no-pain-effects-of-social-exclusion-on-physical
Deloitte. (2015). *The role of diversity practices and inclusion in promoting trust and employee engagement*. Deloitte Australia. https://www.deloitte.com/au/en/services/consulting/perspectives/role-diversity-practices-inclusion-trust-employee-engagement.html
Deloitte. (2023a). Asia Pacific Impact Report 2023: People. Retrieved from https://www.deloitte.com/au/en/about/governance/asia-pacific-impact-report-people.html
Deloitte. (2023b). *2023 Global human capital trends: New fundamentals for a boundaryless world*. https://www2.deloitte.com/us/en/insights/focus/human-capital-trends/2023/future-of-workforce-management.html

Dillon, B., & Sable, S. (2016). *Inclusive Leadership Framework*. Retrieved from https://www.organizationwebsite.com/framework

Eisenberger, N. I., Lieberman, M. D., & Williams, K. D. (2003). Does rejection hurt? An fMRI study of social exclusion. *Science*, 302(5643), 290–292. https://sanlab.psych.ucla.edu/wp-content/uploads/sites/31/2016/03/Eisenberger-Lieberman-Williams-2003-Science.pdf

Ernst & Young. (n.d.). *Four tips to managing four generations in one workforce.* Forbes. Retrieved March 6, 2025, from https://www.forbes.com/sites/forbeshumanresourcescouncil/2017/11/01/four-tips-to-managing-four-generations-in-one-workforce

Eurich, T. (2017). *Insight: The surprising truth about how others see us, how we see ourselves, and why the answers matter more than we think.* Crown Business.

Eurich, T. (2018, January). What self-awareness really is (and how to cultivate it). *Harvard Business Review.* https://hbr.org/2018/01/what-self-awareness-really-is-and-how-to-cultivate-it

Field, E., Hancock, B., Smallets, S., & Weddle, B. (2023, June 26). Investing in middle managers pays off—literally. McKinsey & Company. https://www.mckinsey.com/capabilities/people-and-organizational-performance/our-insights/investing-in-middle-managers-pays-off-literally

Finlay, L. (2002). *"Negotiating the swamp: The opportunity and challenge of reflexivity in research practice."* Qualitative Research, 2(2), 209–230.

Forrester Consulting. (2021). *The business impact of investing in experience: A spotlight on experience-driven businesses.* Adobe. https://business.adobe.com/content/dam/dx/us/en/resources/reports/the-business-impact-of-investing-in-experience-forrester-thought-leadership-paper-2021/the-business-impact-of-investing-in-experience-forrester-thought-leadership-paper-2021.pdf

Fraser-Thill, R., & Gopal, S. (2023, March 27). *How to talk to your team about their career development.* Harvard Business Review. https://hbsp.harvard.edu/product/H07JYJ-PDF-ENG

Gable, S. L., Reis, H. T., Impett, E. A., & Asher, E. R. (2004). *What do you do when things go right? The intrapersonal and interpersonal benefits of sharing positive events.* Journal of Personality and Social Psychology, 87(2), 228–245. https://doi.org/10.1037/0022-3514.87.2.228

Gabrieli, G., Esposito, G., & Truzzi, A. (2018, July). Promoting empathy with rhymes: Effects of poetry exposure on physiological arousal and empathic trait. Paper presented at the European Society for Cognitive and Affective Neuroscience (ESCAN) Conference, Leiden, Netherlands.

Gallup. (2023, June 13). *The $8.8 trillion workplace problem: Gallup's State of the Global Workplace 2023 report.* https://www.gallup.com/workplace/393497/world-trillion-workplace-problem.aspx

Gallwey, W. T. (2000). *The inner game of work.* Random House.

Ganczarek J, Hünefeldt T, Olivetti Belardinelli M. From "Einfühlung" to empathy: exploring the relationship between aesthetic and interpersonal experience. Cogn Process. 2018 May;19(2):141–145. https://doi.org/10.1007/s10339-018-0861-x. Epub 2018 May 15. PMID: 29766344; PMCID: PMC5976702.

Gartner. (n.d.). *Workforce diversity: What it is and why it matters*. Retrieved March 30, 2025, from https://www.gartner.com/en/human-resources/trends/workforce-diversity

Gielan, M. (2015). *Broadcasting happiness: The science of igniting and sustaining positive change*. BenBella Books.

Goleman, D., Boyatzis, R., & McKee, A. (2002). Primal leadership: Unleashing the power of emotional intelligence. Harvard Business Review Press.

Goleman, D. (1998). Working with emotional intelligence. Bantam Books.

Goleman, D. (1995). Emotional intelligence: Why it can matter more than IQ. Bantam Books

Goldsmith, M., & Reiter, M. (2007). What got you here won't get you there: How successful people become even more successful. Hyperion.

Goldsmith, M. (2010). Mojo: How to get it, how to keep it, how to get it back if you lose it. Hyperion.

Google. (2024). *Diversity annual report 2024*. https://belonging.google/diversity-annual-report/2024/

Gottman, J. M. (1994). *Why marriages succeed or fail: And how you can make yours last*. Simon & Schuster.

Grant, A. M. (2012). An integrated model of goal-focused coaching: An evidence-based framework for teaching and practice. *International Coaching Psychology Review, 7*(2), 146–165.

Great Place to Work. (2023, August 31). *Companies that care 2023*. https://www.greatplacetowork.com/companies-that-care

Higher Education Recruitment Consortium. (n.d.). *About HERC*. Retrieved April 1, 2025, from https://www.hercjobs.org/about/

Helgesen, S. (2023). *Rising together: How we can bridge divides and create a more inclusive workplace*. Hachette Go.

Hess, E. D., & Ludwig, K. (2017). Humility is the new smart: Rethinking human excellence in the smart machine age. Berrett-Koehler Publishers.

Horan, J. (2013a). Moments of realization: A cross-cultural narrative inquiry into leadership [Doctoral dissertation, University of Bristol].

Horan, J. (2013b). *Words collide; mindsets remain*. In S. Trahar (Ed.), *Contextualising narrative inquiry: Developing methodological approaches for local context* (pp. 178–194). Routledge.

Horan, J. (2014). How Asian women lead: Lessons for global corporations. Palgrave Macmillan.

Horan, J. (2018). Now it's clear: The career you own. Springtime Books.

Institute of Management Accountants. (2022). *Global perspectives on talent retention in the accounting and finance profession: Asia-Pacific focus*. https://web.iaiglobal.or.id/assets/files/file_berita/IMAGlobalTalentRetentionReport asiapacificFinal.pdf

International Coaching Federation. (2024). *2024 ICF technology in coaching survey: Summary report*. https://coachingfederation.org

International Dual Career Network. (n.d.). *About IDCN*. Retrieved March 6, 2025, from https://idcn.info/about-idcn

Jenkins, J. A. (2016). *Disrupt aging: A bold new path to living your best life at every age*. PublicAffairs.

Kahneman, D. (2011). Thinking, fast and slow. Farrar, Straus and Giroux.

Kahneman, D., & Tversky, A. (1974). Judgment under uncertainty: Heuristics and biases. Science, 185(4157), 1124–1131. https://doi.org/10.1126/science.185.4157.1124

Kaye, B., & Giulioni, J. W. (2024). *Help them grow or watch them go: Career conversations organizations need and employees still want* (3rd ed.). Berrett-Koehler Publishers.

Kidd, D. C., & Castano, E. (2013). Reading literary fiction improves theory of mind. Science, 342(6156), 377–380. https://doi.org/10.1126/science.1239918

Kim, P. T. (2017). Data-driven discrimination at work. *William & Mary Law Review, 58*(3), 857–936. https://scholarship.law.wm.edu/wmlr/vol58/iss3/3

Kline, N. (1999). *Time to think: Listening to ignite the human mind*. Cassell.

Kline, N. (2009). More time to think: A way of being in the world. Fisher King Publishing.

Kline, N. (2023). *I Promise Not to Interrupt: Building Thinking Environments for Real Conversations*. Penguin Business.

Konrath S, Martingano AJ, Davis M, Breithaupt F. Empathy trends in American youth between 1979 and 2018: an update. Soc Psychol Personal Sci. Published online December 28, 2023. https://doi.org/10.1177/19485506231218360

Kouzes, J. M., & Posner, B. Z. (1987). *The leadership challenge: How to get extraordinary things done in organizations*. Jossey-Bass.

Krznaric, R. (2014). Empathy: Why it matters, and how to get it. TarcherPerigee.

Lally, P., Van Jaarsveld, C. H. M., Potts, H. W. W., & Wardle, J. (2009). How are habits formed: Modelling habit formation in the real world. *European Journal of Social Psychology, 40*(6), 998–1009. https://doi.org/10.1002/ejsp.674

LEGO Group. (2020, June 15). *The LEGO Group to invest up to US$400 million over three years to accelerate sustainability efforts*. https://www.lego.com/en-us/aboutus/news/2020/june/sustainability-investment

LinkedIn Learning. (2025). *Workplace learning report*. LinkedIn. https://learning.linkedin.com/resources/workplace-learning-report

Lobel, O. (2022). *The equality machine: Harnessing digital technology for a brighter, more inclusive future*. PublicAffairs.

Lorenzo, R., Voigt, N., Tsusaka, M., Krentz, M., & Abouzahr, K. (2018, January 23). *How diverse leadership teams boost innovation*. Boston Consulting Group. https://www.bcg.com/publications/2018/how-diverse-leadership-teams-boost-innovation

Losada, M., & Heaphy, E. (2004). The Role of Positivity and Connectivity in the Performance of Business Teams: A Nonlinear Dynamics Model. American Behavioral Scientist, 47(6), 740–765. https://doi.org/10.1177/0002764203260208

Ligorner, K. L., & Zhu, Y. (2024, September 19). *China announces plan to gradually increase statutory retirement age*. Morgan Lewis. https://www.morganlewis.com/pubs/2024/09/china-announces-plan-to-gradually-increase-statutory-retirement-age

Maister, D. H., Green, C. H., & Galford, R. M. (2000). *The trusted advisor*. Free Press.

McKinsey & Company, & Lean In. (2023). *Women in the workplace 2023*. https://www.mckinsey.com/featured-insights/diversity-and-inclusion/women-in-the-workplace

McKinsey & Company. (2025). *Superagency in the workplace: Empowering people to unlock AI's full potential*. https://www.mckinsey.com/capabilities/mckinsey-digital/our-insights/superagency-in-the-workplace-empowering-people-to-unlock-ais-full-potential-at-work

McLeod, S. (2015, November). *Do great leaders really need self-awareness?* World Economic Forum. https://www.weforum.org/stories/2015/11/do-great-leaders-really-need-self-awareness/

McNeil, L., & Sher, M. (1999). The dual-career-couple problem. *Physics Today*, 52(7), 32–37. https://doi.org/10.1063/1.882658

Meyer, E. (2014). *The culture map: Breaking through the invisible boundaries of global business*. PublicAffairs.

Organisation for Economic Co-operation and Development. (2024). *Society at a glance 2024: OECD social indicators*. OECD Publishing. https://doi.org/10.1787/918d8db3-en

O'Neil, C. (2016). *Weapons of math destruction: How big data increases inequality and threatens democracy*. Crown Publishing Group.

Palmer, P. J. (2004). *A hidden wholeness: the journey toward an undivided life: welcoming the soul and weaving community in a wounded world*. San Francisco, CA, Jossey-Bass.

Parker, P., & Arthur, M. B. (2004). *Giving voice to the dual-career couple.* British Journal of Guidance & Counselling, 32(1), 3–23. eurekamag.com+4cliffsno tes.com+4link.springer.com+4

Permits Foundation. (2022). *International dual careers survey report.* Retrieved from https://www.permitsfoundation.com/wp-content/uploads/2022/10/Oct_13_2022_Partner_Survey_Report_Final.pdf

Rai, T., & Dutkiewicz, C. (2022, May 10). *How to navigate pushback to diversity, equity and inclusion efforts.* Gartner. https://www.gartner.com/en/articles/how-to-navigate-pushback-to-diversity-equity-and-inclusion-efforts

Reyes, V., Ashton, H., & Moutray, C. (2021). *Creating pathways for tomorrow's workforce today: Beyond reskilling in manufacturing.* Deloitte Insights. https://www2.deloitte.com/us/en/insights/industry/manufacturing/manufacturing-industry-diversity.html

Riess H. The Science of Empathy. J Patient Exp. 2017 Jun;4(2):74–77. https://doi.org/10.1177/2374373517699267. Epub 2017 May 9. PMID: 28725865; PMCID: PMC5513638.

Robbins, J. (2021, January 5). *How long does it really take to form a habit?* Scientific American. https://www.scientificamerican.com/article/how-long-does-it-really-take-to-form-a-habit/

Rocky.ai. (n.d.). *Rocky: AI coach for personal development.* Retrieved April 1, 2025, from https://www.rocky.ai/

Schein, E. H., & Schein, P. A. (2018). Humble leadership: The power of relationships, openness, and trust. Berrett-Koehler Publishers.

Schein, E. H., & Schein, P. A. (2017). *Organizational culture and leadership* (5th ed.). Hoboken, NJ: Wiley.

Schiebinger, L., Henderson, A. D., & Gilmartin, S. K. (2008). *Dual-career academic couples: What universities need to know.* Stanford University, Michelle R. Clayman Institute for Gender Research. https://gender.stanford.edu/sites/gender/files/dualcareerfinal_0.pdf

Singapore Department of Statistics. (2020). *Census of population 2020: Statistical release 2 - Findings on households, geographic distribution, transport and difficulty in activities of daily living.* https://www.singstat.gov.sg/-/media/files/publications/cop2020/sr2/findings2.pdf

Solis-Moreira, J. & Young, L. (2024, January 24). *How long does it really take to form a habit? Scientific American.* https://www.scientificamerican.com/article/how-long-does-it-really-take-to-form-a-habit/

Sotirin, P., & Goltz, S. M. (2019). Academic dual career as a lifeworld orientation: A phenomenological inquiry. *The Review of Higher Education, 42*(3), 1207–1232. https://doi.org/10.1353/rhe.2019.0034

Statista Research Department. (2023). *Number of dual-income households in Japan from 2014 to 2023 (in millions).* Statista. https://www.statista.com/statistics/857228/japan-dual-income-households/

TechTarget. (2025, February 27). *U.S. companies scale back DEI initiatives under new federal directive*. https://www.techtarget.com/searchhrsoftware/news/366568899/US-companies-scale-back-DEI-initiatives-under-new-federal-directive

Temple, C. N. (2010). Sankofa: Celebrating the past to awaken the future. *The Journal of Pan African Studies, 3*(10), 127–142.

Tozzi, J. (2022, February 12). *IBM emails show millennial workers favored over 'dinobabies'*. Bloomberg. https://www.bloomberg.com/news/articles/2022-02-12/ibm-emails-show-millennial-workers-favored-over-dinobabies

The Guardian. (2021, March 2). Unconscious bias training alone will not stop discrimination, say critics. Retrieved from https://www.theguardian.com/money/2021/mar/02/unconscious-bias-training-alone-will-not-stop-discrimination-say-critics#:~:text=While%20studies%20have%20repeatedly%20shown,diversity%20objectives%2C%E2%80%9D%20Newry%20said

Tofade T, Elsner J, Haines ST. Best practice strategies for effective use of questions as a teaching tool. Am J Pharm Educ. 2013 Sep 12;77(7):155. https://doi.org/10.5688/ajpe777155. PMID: 24052658; PMCID: PMC3776909.

Trompenaars, F., & Hampden-Turner, C. (2012). *Riding the waves of culture: Understanding diversity in global business* (3rd ed.). McGraw-Hill.

University of Florida. (2018, July 19). *Most patients get just 11 seconds to explain reason for visit before they are interrupted*. ScienceDaily. https://www.sciencedaily.com/releases/2018/07/180719112209.htm

Valcour, M. (2014, April 17). *Why managers don't have career conversations*. Harvard Business Review. https://hbr.org/2014/04/why-managers-dont-have-career-conversations

Van Tongeren, D. R. (n.d.). The transformative power of humility. Templeton Foundation. Retrieved January 8, 2025, from https://www.templeton.org/news/the-transformative-power-of-humility

Visier. (2020, February 3). *New research finds people analytics helps organizations increase gender diversity in leadership*. Retrieved from https://www.visier.com/company/news/new-research-people-analytics-increase-gender-diversity-leadership/

Wasburn, M. H. (1999). The dual-career-couple problem: A type of exclusion that affects women disproportionately. *Physics Today, 52*(7), 32–37. https://doi.org/10.1063/1.882861

Wetherell, E., & Nelson, B. (2021, August 12). 8 practical tips for leaders for a better onboarding process. Gallup. Retrieved from https://www.gallup.com/workplace/354066/practical-tips-leaders-better-onboarding-process.aspx

Whitelaw, G. (2012). *The Zen leader: 10 ways to go from barely managing to leading fearlessly*. Nicholas Brealey Publishing.

Williams, K. D. (2007). Cyberball: A program for use in research on interpersonal ostracism and acceptance. Behavior Research Methods, 39(2), 277–289. https://link.springer.com/article/10.3758/BF03192765

Woolsey, M. (2024, July 5). Want to keep staff on side? It's not rocket science. The Times. Retrieved from https://www.thetimes.com/business-money/companies/article/want-to-keep-staff-on-side-its-not-rocket-science-zvtgnf0hx

World Economic Forum. (2023). *Zero Health Gap Pledge: Global Health Equity Network.* https://initiatives.weforum.org/global-health-equity-network/pledge

Xu, S. (2019) A Review of the Effectiveness and Boundary Conditions of Leader Humility. Journal of Service Science and Management, 12, 234–245. https://doi.org/10.4236/jssm.2019.122016

Zaki, J. (2019). The war for kindness: Building empathy in a fractured world. Crown Publishing Group.

Zenger, J., & Folkman, J. (2015, November 4). *We like leaders who underrate themselves.* Harvard Business Review. https://hbr.org/2015/11/we-like-leaders-who-underrate-themselves

Zheng, W., Kim, J., Kark, R., & Mascolo, L. (2023, September 27). *What makes an inclusive leader.* Harvard Business Review. https://hbr.org/2023/09/what-makes-an-inclusive-leader

CHART ON ASIA RETIREMENT AGE

SINGAPORE

Ministry of Manpower Singapore. (n.d.). Retirement and re-employment in Singapore. Retrieved from https://www.mom.gov.sg/employment-practices/retirement-and-re-employment

MALAYSIA

OECD. (2024a). Pensions at a Glance Asia/Pacific 2024: Malaysia. Retrieved from https://www.oecd.org/en/publications/pensions-at-a-glance-asia-pacific-2024_d4146d12-en/full-report/malaysia_06aca9d1.html

CHINA

Baker McKenzie. (2024, October 9). China extends statutory retirement age – What does this mean for employers? Retrieved from https://insightplus.bakermckenzie.com/bm/pensions_10/china-china-extends-statutory-retirement-age-what-does-this-mean-for-employers

Japan

OECD. (2024b). Pensions at a Glance Asia/Pacific 2024: Japan. Retrieved from https://www.oecd.org/en/publications/pensions-at-a-glance-asia-pacific-2024_d4146d12-en/full-report/japan_59a40147.html

China Data: English Citation

National Civil Service Administration. (2020). Provisions on recruitment of civil servants. Retrieved from http://www.scs.gov.cn/zcfg/202001/t20200108_16198.html

Chinese Citation with English Translation

国家公务员局. (2020). 公务员录用规定 [Provisions on recruitment of civil servants]. 国家公务员局. Retrieved from http://www.scs.gov.cn/zcfg/202001/t20200108_16198.html

Data on Dual Career Households

Singapore

Singapore Department of Statistics. (2021). *Census of Population 2020: Statistical Release 2 - Households, Geographic Distribution, Transport and Difficulty in Basic Activities*. Retrieved from https://www.singstat.gov.sg/-/media/files/publications/cop2020/sr2/cop2020sr2.pdf

Japan

Statista. (2023). *Number of dual income households in Japan from 2014 to 2023 (in millions)*. Retrieved from https://www.statista.com/statistics/857228/japan-dual-income-households/

United States

Organisation for Economic Co-operation and Development (OECD). (2022). *OECD Economic Surveys: United States 2022*. Retrieved from https://www.oecd.org/economy/surveys/United-States-2022-OECD-economic-survey-overview.pdf

European Union

Organisation for Economic Co-operation and Development (OECD). (2021). *LMF2.2: Patterns of employment and the distribution of working hours among couple families*. Retrieved from https://www.oecd.org/els/family/LMF2_2_Patterns_of_employment_distribution_of_working_hours_couple_families.pdf

Work Visa Information Japan, U.S. and EU

Japan: Dependent Visas

Ministry of Foreign Affairs of Japan. (n.d.). *General visa: Dependent (family stays)*. Retrieved April 1, 2025, from https://www.mofa.go.jp/j_info/visit/visa/long/visa9.html

United States: H-4 Visa Employment Authorization

U.S. Citizenship and Immigration Services. (n.d.). *Employment authorization for certain H-4 dependent spouses*. Retrieved April 1, 2025, from https://www.uscis.gov/working-in-the-united-states/temporary-workers/h-1b-specialty-occupations/employment-authorization-for-certain-h-4-dependent-spouses

Europe: Family Members' Residence Rights

European Commission. (n.d.). *Your non-EU spouse and children's residence rights in the EU*. Retrieved April 1, 2025, from https://europa.eu/youreurope/citizens/residence/family-residence-rights/non-eu-wife-husband-children/index_en.htm

Previous Publications

Books

I Wish I'd Known That Earlier in My Career: The Power of Positive Workplace Politics (2012)
How Asian Women Lead: Lessons for Global Corporations (2014)
Now It's Clear: The Career You Own (2017)

Academic Contributions

"Creative Non-Fiction Across Cultures in Asia Pacific Contexts," in *Using Narrative Inquiry for Educational Research in the Asia Pacific* (Routledge, 2015)

"Words Collide, Mindsets Remain: A Narrative Inquiry," in *Contextualising Narrative Inquiry: Developing Methodological Approaches for Local Contexts* (Routledge, 2013)

ADDITIONAL WRITING

Author of over 100 articles on Medium, focusing on inclusion, leadership, and career development.

Index

A
Active listening, 4, 76, 147. *See also* Thinking Environment
Adaptive Career Coaching Process, 94, 191
Ageism, 98, 101–105
  age 35 phenomena, 101
  impact on women, 101
  steps to address, 103
AI
  AI-powered platforms (AIMY, RockyAI, ChatGPT), 175, 178
  AI-powered tool questions to consider, 172
  bias in AI, 180
  Where AI falls short, 196
Anchoring bias, 24
Archer, Margaret, 171
Arthur, Michael, 118, 123, 124, 126
Availability bias, 24

B
Bachkirova, Tatiana, 177–179
Behavioral change, 146, 156, 158, 159, 167, 168, 170, 172, 179. *See also* Leadership behaviors
Belonging, x, 16, 31, 135, 156, 164
Benson, Buster, 25
BetterUp, 169
Burns, James McGregor, 155, 171
Burt, Ron, 57, 58, 61

C
Carboni, Inga, 57, 62, 72, 73
Career conversations
  impact, 94, 99, 102, 105
  myths, 96
Clutterbuck, David, 165, 166, 178, 179
  Coaching Levels and Impact (with Megginson), 165
Coaching
  for behavioral change, 156, 158, 159, 167, 168, 170, 179
  measuring the impact, 170
  process (empathy), 15, 40, 83, 86, 124, 127, 178, 180, 184

Conviction coaching questions, 20
Conviction in inclusive leadership, 18
Corporate culture, 4, 19, 44, 78, 148
Cross, Rob, 57, 72
Cultural sensitivity, 32
Culture change, 128, 149, 150

D
DeWall, Nathan, 16
Dillon, Bernadette, 27
Dual-career couples
  academics, 112
  implementing dual-career coaching, 127
  MNCs, 122
  NGOs, 109, 113, 116, 118
  reshaping policy (Boston Consulting Group), 124
  two-body problem, 112, 113

E
Eisenberger, Naomi, 16
Empathy
  coaching questions, 20
  cornerstone of inclusion, 45
  deficit, 43, 45
  empathy in action, 39
  roots, 47
  science (emotional and cognitive), 41
  six habits, 40
Employee engagement, 79, 96, 159, 171
Empowerment, 18, 86
Exclusion, 5, 6, 9, 12, 13, 16, 32, 34, 62, 135, 156, 164, 182
  cost of, 70, 71

F
Facilitation, 178, 181

Fairness, 4, 49, 103, 163, 195
Favoritism, 36
Feedback loops, 87, 184
Finlay, Linda, 171
Folkman, Joseph, 5, 30, 32, 150

G
Gable, Shelly, 35
Gallwey, Tim, 94
Global talent, 7, 87, 113, 115
Goldsmith, Marshall, 45, 56, 158
  4C method, 35
Goleman, Daniel, 61, 170
Goltz, Sonia, 113
Gottman, John, 35, 85
Grant, Anthony, 169

H
Halpern, Diane, 61
Hampden-Turner, Charles, 23
Heaphy, Emily, 35
Helgesen, Sally, 74
Hess, Edward, 50, 52
Human connection, 172, 175, 176, 184, 196
Humility
  across cultures, 49–51, 53
  and Hogan Leadership Series, 50
  and networks, 7, 58, 59
  and organizational culture, 50, 51, 53
  here and now (Schein), 185
  Is the New Smart, 52

I
Impact of inclusion, 5, 147, 159
Inclusion, as a strategic imperative
  and belonging, 30, 164
  behavioral change timeframe, 167
  building inclusive leaders, 166
  measuring coaching impact, 170

Inclusive Leadership Compass
  Framework (ILC)
  coaching and peer learning circles,
    134
  focus areas (Self, Others, Team,
    Organization), 52, 67, 84
  measuring impact, 146
  organizational cultural change, 6,
    128
Inclusive talent management, 62, 73,
  86, 190
Innovation and inclusion, 151
Intelligent Career Card System
  (ICCS)
  coaching sample, 111, 120
  Knowing Why, Knowing How,
    Knowing Whom, 192
International Coaching Federation
  (ICF), 168, 178, 182

K
Kahneman, Daniel, 24, 26
Kaye, Beverly, 89, 96–98, 104
Kemp, Rob, 177–179
Kim, Pauline, 8
Kline, Nancy. *See* Thinking
  Environment
Krznaric, Roman, 40, 43, 47, 48

L
Langowitz, Nan, 62
Leadership behaviors
  behavioral shifts, 146, 195
  measuring, 30
Leadership development and AI, 156,
  172, 173, 181, 196
Leadership frameworks, 5, 24, 68, 73
Leadership styles, 23, 63, 73, 74, 78,
  87, 190
Leaders' perspectives on inclusion and
  coaching, 155, 194

Listening. *See* Thinking Environment
Lobel, Orly, 8, 9, 180, 182
Losada, Marcial, 35
Ludwig, Katherine, 52

M
Maister, David, 78–81, 83, 84, 135,
  166
Manoogian, John III, 25
Measuring impact, 146. *See also*
  Coaching; Inclusion, as a
  strategic imperative
Mentoring, 90, 99, 105, 157, 163,
  195
Meyer, Erin, 23
Mid- to late-career professionals, 87,
  105–107
Mutual exchange (for measuring
  impact), 171

N
Networks
  and inclusion, 59, 61, 62, 68
  mapping exclusion, 62

O
Onboarding for inclusion, 67, 68, 71,
  86
O'Neil, Cathy, 180
Organizational culture change
  culture and ILC assessments, 147
  measuring impact, 146
  questions instead of solutions, 143
  shifting mindsets, 145
  team shifts, 141
  Thinking Council to drive change,
    143
Organizational Network Analysis
  (ONA), 61–63, 72, 86, 190
Organizational systems, 43

P

Parker, Andrew, 62
Parker, Polly, 123, 124, 126
Perception management, 7, 58, 60, 62
Psychological safety, 15, 31, 196

R

Reflective practice, 162, 178
Reflexivity, 170, 171, 177
Relationship building, 26, 47, 178
Rilke, Rainer Maria, 186

S

Sable, Sandy, 27
Schein, Edgar, 49, 50, 52, 53, 57, 58, 63, 142, 171, 185
Self-awareness, 6, 14, 29, 31, 37, 38, 40, 43, 45, 49, 63, 132, 137, 139, 147, 157, 165, 166, 172, 185–187, 196
  coaching questions, 20, 34
Shifting mindsets, 145
Societal impact, 4, 161
Sotirin, Patty, 113
Stakeholder feedback, 34, 37
Stakeholder interviews, 34, 53, 74, 77, 83, 171, 195
Structural inequities, 8

T

Talent management (inclusive), 62, 73, 86, 190
Talent retention, 79, 151

Thinking Environment
  coaching, 15, 31, 78, 87
  10 Components and inclusion, 81
  inclusive meetings, 83
  questions instead of solutions, 143, 145
  Thinking Council (driving inclusive culture), 134, 142, 143, 145, 146, 189, 193
Transformational leadership, 4
Trompenaars, Fons, 23
Tversky, Amos, 24

U

Unconscious bias, 23, 24, 30, 62

V

Van Tongeren, Daryl, 50

W

Well-Being and Engagement Framework (WBEF) to measure impact, 169
Why inclusion matters, 164
Williams, Kipling D., 16

X

Xu, Shang, 50, 51

Z

Zaki, Jamil, 40, 43, 45, 48
Zenger, Jack, 5, 30, 32, 150

The manufacturer's authorised representative in the EU is Springer
Nature Customer Service Centre GmbH, Europaplatz 3, 69115 Heidelberg,
Germany. If you have any concerns regarding our products, please
contact ProductSafety@springernature.com

Printed and bound by CPI Group (UK) Ltd, Croydon, CR0 4YY
20/04/2026
02093298-0001